a short &happy guide to
Being a College Student

A Daily Companion for School, Work and Life

by

Paula A. Franzese
Peter W. Rodino Professor of Law
Seton Hall Law School

Creator and Editor of the Short and Happy Series

Mat #41581659

Short and Happy Guide Series is a trademark registered in the U.S. Patent and Trademark Office.

© 2014 LEG, Inc. d/b/a West Academic

    444 Cedar Street, Suite 700
    St. Paul, MN 55101
    1-877-888-1330

Printed in the United States of America

ISBN: 978-0-314-29138-7

For Michael Luigi and Nina Paula, the song in my heart.

Preface

This book began as a set of letters that I wrote to my son Michael as he was about to begin Boston College. In the months leading up to his departure, and in part to help with my own worry and sadness at the idea of letting him go, I would write him a letter a day, and leave the letter on his dresser. The letters contained advice, inspiration and reminders of the mightiness of his destiny. They represented everything that I wanted him to know as he entered this next phase of his life. As the letters piled up, my son said, *"Mom, you should write a book."* This is that book.

I am a law professor and public interest lawyer. First and foremost, I am a mother. I know the struggles and triumphs of the learning process, the anxieties of social interactions and the pressures to fit in. This book was written with great love to provide reassurance, guidance and wisdom, particularly at those moments when our children find themselves at a crossroads. We make bad choices because we forget. In these pages are reminders for all of our children—reminders of how deeply they are cherished and how precious they are, reminders that God has chosen to do great works through them and reminders to keep that big vision directly in front of every decision that they make.

In the Property, Commercial Law, Civil Rights and Civil Liberties and First Amendment Values courses that I teach, I am continuously inspired by the generosity and kindness of my students. Because of their goodness, I have also come to teach about hope, compassion, being proud of who you are and where you come from, the call to service and our responsibility as healers. I am grateful that my message has struck a responsive chord.

This book endeavors to allay some of the fears that school, work and life can conjure up. It is a reminder to include goodness and kindness in everything that we do. Education can sometimes divorce humanity and our own humanness from the study of the subject matter at hand. That tendency is tragic.

When we separate virtue from learning we miss the point. When we hide or segment off whole aspects of our selves to become something we think we are supposed to be we lose our integrity. The very word *"integrity"* comes from the Latin *integritas*, meaning wholeness. We live and learn with integrity when we are able to integrate the pursuit of excellence with the steadfast commitment to decency. We practice integrity when we respect intelligence, but respect kindness more.

A good education can take its beneficiaries to great heights. But no matter the altitude, I ask my children and my students to always be mindful of the legacy of virtue that preceded them. I encourage them to reject complacency and cynicism and to accept their role as healers. We are all healers. We heal with our words and with our actions. We heal with one kind thought and one generous impulse rendered one day at a time. We heal when we resolve to love the process of learning, and to treat it as if we love it. We heal when we love the communities that we are lucky enough to serve. We heal when we finally decide to love ourselves so much that the spillover cannot help but bring joy to the world.

This book was inspired by and written with great love. My children are the joy of my life and my students are shining lights. I thank them for the privilege.

Paula A. Franzese

February, 2014

About the Author

Paula A. Franzese, the Peter W. Rodino Professor of Law at Seton Hall Law School, is the creator and editor of the *Short and Happy Guide* series, and is the author of *A Short and Happy Guide to Property* and *A Short and Happy Guide to Being a Law Student*. Nationally renowned for her excellence in teaching, she is the unprecedented ten-time recipient of the Student Bar Association's Professor of the Year Award, has been named "Exemplary Teacher" by the American Association of Higher Education and most recently was named one of only 26 "best law teachers in the United States." The book, *What the Best Law Teachers Do* (Harvard University Press), profiles in detail the pedagogical approach that renders her a "dazzlingly effective model of rigor, hard work, creativity and humility". Prof. Franzese has demonstrated and deconstructed her pedagogical expertise on teaching as both art and science at workshops and colloquia across the country. She is the Gilbert's *"Legend of the Law"* in Property (West audio series), the national Property lecturer for the BAR/BRI bar review course, the author of the book *Strategies and Techniques for Teaching Property* (Walters Kluwer) and a contributor to the books *America's Second Gilded Age? Perspectives on Law and Class Differences* (NYU Press), *The Affective Assistance of Counsel: Practicing Law as a Healing Profession* (Carolina Academic Press), and *Reaction and Reform in New Jersey* (Hall Institute).

Prof. Franzese's scholarship in the area of Property law includes critical examination of common interest communities, homeowners associations and the dilemma of privatization, the law of servitudes, exclusionary zoning, affordable housing, adverse possession doctrine and takings law. She joined in the submission to the U.S. Supreme Court of an *amicus* brief in the *Kelo* Case, and has written and presented on takings law reform. She is a Fellow of the American College of Real Estate Lawyers, a Fellow of the

American Bar Foundation and the recipient of numerous accolades, including the Sir Thomas More Medal of Honor, the YWCA Woman of Influence Award, the Women Lawyers Association's Trailblazer Award, and the State Bar Foundation's Medal of Honor.

As one of the country's leading experts in property law as well as government ethics, Prof. Franzese has spearheaded ethics reform initiatives on behalf of three governors, serving as Special Ethics Counsel to Governor Richard Codey, Chair of the State Ethics Commission, Vice-Chair of the Election Law Enforcement Commission and as ethics advisor to state and local governments across the country, including Mayor Cory Booker's administration in Newark. Among her initiatives in those arenas, she and Justice Daniel J. O'Hern promulgated the Uniform Ethics Code, a pioneering statutory achievement that has become a model for national replication. In recognition of her accomplishments, Prof. Franzese was presented with the National Council on Governmental Ethics Laws (COGEL) Award, the highest form of recognition conferred by the organization, in honor of her "significant, demonstrable and positive contributions to the fields of campaign finance, elections, ethics, freedom of information and lobbying over a significant period of time."

Professor Franzese was a litigator with Cahill, Gordon and Reindel in New York City, where she also served as a member of the New York Housing Court Reform Project and the Governor's Task Force on Life and Law. She clerked for Justice Alan B. Handler of the New Jersey Supreme Court. She received her B.A., *summa cum laude*, Phi Beta Kappa, from Barnard College, Columbia University, where she was awarded the Bryson Prize, Alpha Zeta Fellowship, Marion Churchill White Prize, Davidson-Foreman Foundation Award and Barnard Alumnae Fellowship, and her J.D. from Columbia University School of Law, where she was an International Fellow, Teaching Fellow and recipient of the prestigious Rosenman Prize for excellence in public law courses.

Table of Contents

A Short & Happy Guide to Being a College Student

Introduction

Why and When to Read This Book.

We are all students. The rigors of school, work and life can be exhilarating, but the challenges can bring moments of doubt, even for the most self-assured. Particularly at the start of any new venture, whether in a new school or at a new job, people who are accustomed to feeling competent and successful can suddenly find themselves questioning their abilities and their place in unfamiliar territory. The night before I was to begin law school, I remember phoning home in a panic. I still had more than fifty pages to read, and I could not understand most of it. Tired and overwhelmed, I cried to my dad, *"I'm terrified. I don't think that the law is for me. I can't do this."* My father replied, "Paolina" (his pet name for me, which translated from Italian is said to mean "little legal genius of our nation," although that may be a loose translation), *"Throw your fears out the window. For this moment, stop thinking with your weary mind and go to what you know in your heart. You are precisely where you are meant to be."* Then my dad added three words that I have invoked on many occasions since: *"GO TO SLEEP!"*

Most fears are born of fatigue, and a good night's rest is often curative. This book is meant to be a nightstand companion whenever anxiety or dread starts to creep in and whenever the voices of the naysayers *("You can't do this," "It's too hard," "What's the point?")* start to take up space in your head. Make one of its chapters the last thing you read before turning in for the night. Make parts of it the first thing you read upon rising. It contains messages of hope and it will remind you of the mightiness of your mission and the magnitude of your abilities.

We suffer because we forget. Remember who you are and where you come from. Your parents, grandparents, their parents and ancestors before them struggled, sacrificed and triumphed so that you would have the opportunity to be where you are at this very moment. The hard work has already been done. The table has been set. All you need to do is take your seat, respectfully and with great humility but also with the presence of mind to know that you belong here, you will thrive here, and you will use your life to bear living witness to the legacy of virtue that preceded you.

PART 1

If You Are Lucky Enough to Be in School, Be Excited and Feel Proud

You are one of the select few people on the planet privileged enough to actually be in school. Countless others would give anything to be where you are now. You have been given the opportunity to hone your analytical skills and powers of discernment so that you can and will become a ninja for the good.

CHAPTER 1

Dreams Brought You Here. You Are Now on the Road to Making Them Come True

The world is yours.

Education is the great equalizer and knowledge is power. No matter your beginnings, you are on the road to making your dreams come true. That sets you apart from the countless souls who find themselves stuck by circumstance and life choices. Your world is limitless. Your course is still unwritten and your path is ripe with promise. That promise of a better life may not yet be available to the guy sitting next to you on the train today, or the woman sitting across from you in the laundry room. You are one of the lucky ones. Across the world, countless people will never get the chance that you have now. You are creating something for your sake and for theirs, and it is very good and very important.

Your degree will equip you to use the rule of reason to advance the cause of progress.

No matter what you are studying, with your degree you will have the opportunity to effect change. And change is needed. There is too much brutality in the world. As an educated citizen of the world, you will develop a vocabulary and skill set that will give you credibility and access. Therein resides your chance to be a paradigm shifter, to bring peace where there is acrimony and understanding where there is intolerance. You will learn to use the rule of reason not in pursuit of "win at all costs" ruthlessness but to promote the cause of progress and equal access for all.

The most significant educators and students value the gentler virtues. They know that wisdom and compassion are indivisible.

You do not need to be aggressive or competitive to succeed. Play your game, no one else's. Your true nature is virtuous. If you stray from your true nature to try to become someone or something else, you will lose your way. Stay true to yourself. Continue to value and practice generosity and compassion. Speak to the better instincts of the people who will be coming into your life. The goodness in you is the same goodness in them. By your example, you will help them to remember.

Whenever you come to a crossroads, take the high road. Do not demean yourself by responding to meanness in kind. Believe in the virtue of others, even when they are not showing their virtuous selves. Treat people as they could be, and in time they will meet you there.

You will teach others that kindness comes from strength.

The decision to lead with both your mind and heart won't always be easy. In the days ahead, there will be times of disappointment and disenchantment, when you will feel like an island. Your virtue will sometimes be mistaken for weakness. But you will know better, and by your example you will help others to see that kindness is a show of strength. It takes courage to step away from the crowds and take a stand for what is right. It takes character to stand up for the underdog. In a world where incivility can seem the norm, it takes steadfastness of purpose to refuse to participate in another's attempt to demean or denigrate anyone else. Be firm in your resolve to be the voice of compassion. Decide now who and what you will stand for.

You will decline the opportunity to answer low-mindedness with more of the same. You will take the high road, again and again, knowing that the force of moral authority will rise up to meet you there. From that perch, the change that you want to see in the world will come.

CHAPTER 2

You Are Smart Enough

If you are feeling intimidated by school or a new job, you are most likely presuming that your classmates or colleagues must be so much smarter than you and the material is so difficult that only the smartest people are able to understand it and work with it. All of that is nonsense and you need to get it out of your head right now.

Genius is overrated.

Greatness does not depend on your IQ. There are "brilliant people" devoid of decency and "geniuses" without the guts to get the job done. They find themselves relegated to the ranks of the reviled or forgotten. As we were growing up, my mom told us time and again, *"The smartest is the one who works the hardest."*

Here is the key to success at any venture: repetition. Repetition brings mastery. To become great at writing papers, keep writing papers, working on draft after draft and incorporating the feedback that you get so that each draft becomes better than the one that preceded it. To become great at taking tests, keep taking simulated practice tests, learning from each practice run and becoming self-corrective after each try. To become great at giving speeches, keep giving speeches. To become great at a foreign language, put in the time and practice, practice, practice.

Work hard and push the ball up the mountain one inch at a time. Persist in the commitment to work hard and you will reach the mountaintop and stay there. Not because you were so smart, but because you were smart enough to know that true greatness comes because of your persistence, strength of character and stubborn commitment to the cause of the good.

There is a force that meets good with good. That force will give you the push when you need it and carry you when you grow weary. It is rooting for you, not testing you. It is cheering you on, every step of the way.

Avoid any and all comparisons with others.

What you bring to this pursuit is what only you can bring. The life experiences that led you to this moment are yours alone and they have prepared you well. Comparison is disrespect for yourself and the object of your comparative appraisal. It cannot help but have you thinking that you are *"more than"* or *"less than"* someone else. That sort of conclusion is both presumptuous and false. Do not denigrate your unique glory by comparing it to another's.

Moreover, your snap judgments about another's strengths or weaknesses are most likely wrong. Resist the urge to label people. Kierkegaard got it right when he said, *"If you label me, you negate me."* Stop sizing up your classmates in some misguided attempt to determine where you stand. You are no better and no worse than anyone else. Everyone has a story to tell and something to teach you. You have your own story to tell, and something to teach the world.

The smartest is the one who works the hardest.

You are smart enough to be in every class that you take. At first, some of the material that you are studying will be difficult. Take your time and know that what you are experiencing is what many others are experiencing. Take the offensive and seek out the classmates who seem to know what they are doing. Ask for their help. Study with them. Reach out to the professor and any teaching assistant for the course. Find out what supplementary readings you might do to get up to speed. Go online and watch lectures or listen to podcasts relevant to the material that you are now covering. Leave your ego out of the equation, refuse to be in denial about any difficulties that you are having and find the people and materials that will help to assure your success.

When you start to feel overwhelmed or less than worthy, realize that you are most likely holding yourself to a crazy standard of perfection. Abandon the quest for some brand of nuanced excellence and simply commit to "good enough." As long as your performance in class and on the exam is good enough, you will be fine.

Intelligence is multi-dimensional. You will find your brand of excellence and create your own artistry.

Do not measure your success according to some linear numerical calculation. That one-dimensional marker cannot begin to know your own unique brand of excellence, what it is that you will excel at most and how it is that you will truly shine. As time goes on, you will discover particular aptitudes of yours that you never knew you had. Those are your brand of genius.

To uncover the *virtuoso* inside of you, say yes to every opportunity that school presents, whether in student government, on behalf of a community leadership initiative, in the arts, as an intern, a mentor, a teaching assistant, on the student newspaper, in athletics and the list goes on. Through a process of elimination, you will come to know what makes your heart sing.

To finish the race is to win the race. You do not have to come in first, second or even in the top 99%. The last one to cross the finish line still crosses the finish line. Every finish brings you closer to the dream. Take your time and cross the line.

CHAPTER 3

Ten Reasons to Be Really Happy About School

REASON ONE: No matter what you are studying, you are honing your powers of discernment so that you can and will become a ninja for the good.

Be excited, because you are learning. No matter your ultimate career aspirations, you are preparing to be a game-changer, whether in the arena of social justice, politics, business, consulting, medicine, science, engineering, the arts, diplomacy, journalism, international affairs, health care, human resources and the list goes on. When the naysayers try to conjure up some parade of horribles about the economy or people, refuse to participate in their life-bashing. Walk away with a smile on your face because you know the truth about the person that you are becoming and the contexts that you will serve.

You were brought to this place and time to heal this place and time. You were born with a purpose even mightier than you know right now. Work hard, study hard and ask God to find you where He needs you to be. Then, just show up, and keep showing up. Your willingness to serve with a kind and generous heart will be rewarded again and again.

REASON TWO: You will find meaning in the work that you do.

Your studies will be a pathway to help you to attain every material gain that your heart desires. Most essentially, your education will give you the greatest gift of all—the opportunity to use your knowledge in service to the world. Answering the call to service, in turn, will assure you a life of meaning. That meaning comes when you realize that you are learning and someday will be practicing all that you have learned for a purpose mightier than yourself.

We do not live only for ourselves. You have come to this room to serve the room. You are connected to the whole of humanity and soon you will be uniquely trained to humanize the inhumane and give voice to the silenced.

Your life will grow in meaning as you move away from ego-driven motivations and toward purpose-driven aspirations. You live your life on purpose when you live for the betterment of others. You live a life of honor when you decide to care more about your significance than your success. Be glad because you have committed to a course of study that will afford you success **and** significance.

REASON THREE: You are developing strength of mind and fortitude of spirit so that you can be a giver of hope.

You will use your expertise to come walking into the room just when it seems to the people who need you most that everyone else has walked out. You are honing your intellectual, practical and emotional aptitudes so that your presence on the scene will bring a sigh of relief. Your degree will vest you with an imprimatur of legitimacy, expertise and authority that commands attention. Often with one phone call, one appearance or one meeting you will be able to make things better. Your messages will be heeded. You are growing in stature, using your growing expertise to command the right kind of attention.

Knowledge is power. You use your power responsibly when you decide to be a giver of hope. You are building strength of mind and character so that you will have a platform from which to protect the disempowered from the tyranny of the majority. No matter your professional path, your work will advance the cause of justice because you will have the wisdom to see what needs to be seen and the courage to respond with compassion.

REASON FOUR: Wisdom and compassion are indivisible. You are becoming a virtuous citizen of the world.

Karl Llewellyn, a legal giant and architect of so much of the modern law of Contracts, astutely observed, *"Compassion without technique is a mess. But technique without compassion is a menace."* Every person who has advanced the cause of rightness has done so by committing to the relentless pursuit of excellence as perceived through a loving lens.

History tells of the atrocities committed at the hands of technocrats whose actions were devoid of any moral referent. Your greatness will reside in your capacity to stubbornly adhere to your virtue and generosity as your continue to hone your intellectual acuities. You are becoming a virtuous citizen of the world.

REASON FIVE: As you grow in expertise and stature, you will teach that each of us is no better (or worse) than anyone else.

Arrogance and one-upmanship have no place in your circle of first principles. Avoid comparisons with others. Do not chase dreams that are not your own. Know that everyone has a story to tell and something to teach you. I remember listening to an interview of Bono, the musician and lead singer of the band U-2, on the occasion of his receipt of a lifetime achievement award. He was asked what it felt like to be so great. He answered, *"We're just a bunch of musicians waiting for God to come walking into the room. Only then do we become the instruments for greatness."* You are becoming an instrument for greatness.

REASON SIX: You will learn to honor the art in you, and not you in the art.

Leave your ego at the door because, at bottom, the journey that you are on is not about you alone. It is about the countless people, most still nameless and unknown, who are waiting for you to get on with the task at hand so that the art that is in you might be used to make their lives better. You will experience the joy of giving your expertise in service to others. In so doing, you will bring endless reward, satisfaction and joy to your own life.

REASON SEVEN: You will learn to be governed by what inspires you, rather than what makes you feel small.

Your life will move in the direction of your predominant thoughts. Be vigilant about them. Think often of all that you are thankful for. When a thought that makes you feel bad seeps in, choose another thought. You are learning to harness the power of your mind to think about, talk about and thank about everything that is good, honorable and right with the world and your place in it. You will help the people and constituencies that you serve to be motivated by their dreams rather than diminished by their nightmares.

REASON EIGHT: You will learn to trust that every day you will be found precisely where you need to be.

You will come to know and trust that when you seek to be used for a purpose mightier than yourself, and ask for ways to use your growing expertise to ease the pain of others, you will find yourself where you need to be. There is a force that greets the generous impulse with a sigh of relief and a debt of gratitude.

Decide today that you will use what you are learning to help others. Then watch what happens as you are placed precisely where you need to be.

REASON NINE: You will resolve to love the work that you have to do, and to treat it as if you love it. You will promise yourself that you will persist in that devotion, no matter the disappointments and occasional disenchantments.

Refuse to heed the cynics or the jaded. Do not listen to that voice in your head that sometimes wants to convince you that you cannot do this or that your hard work won't be worth it. That voice is a liar.

Even if you have to fake it until you make it, proclaim out loud today and every day that you love the work that you have to do. Profess your love for school, your job, your classmates, your co-workers and your career aspirations. Your life will mirror your level of rhetoric about it. Your experiences will rise or fall to meet your level of expectations.

When friends and family ask how it is going, reply, *"It is amazing. I am learning so much and building so many skill sets. The people that I am meeting are great people, and I learn from them every day. My teachers are the best. I am developing muscles I never knew I had, and I will use this strength to make the world a better place. I promise you that. I won't let you down, and I am going to make you proud."* They will smile and reply, *"You already are."*

REASON TEN: You will change your life by speaking only good things about it.

Words are powerful. They speak volumes about their speaker and those who choose to heed their messages. They are the predicates to action. Choose your words wisely. Use them to stir the pot of inspiration, motivation and compassion. When friends, classmates or co-workers begin to complain, try to help them to switch up the thought. If it becomes clear that you cannot do that, simply remove yourself from the conversation.

Misery loves company. Refuse to be an accomplice to another's less than worthy words. You are learning to let what you say facilitate tolerance, understanding and hopefulness. Be excited about this day, because it is bringing you one step closer to the life of your dreams.

CHAPTER 4

The Day I Fell in Love with the Power of a Good Education

Committing to the greater good.

I spent so many years in school and I worked hard, sometimes not knowing whether that effort would be worth it. When I was in college and law school, I remember studying on Saturday nights when my friends from high school were out partying. Sometimes I wondered if life was passing me by. With time, I came to know that life was right there all along, gently whispering, *"Keep at it. Your studies are preparing you to do important work in the world. There are people whose lives will be better because of you. They are as yet nameless and unknown to you, but soon their stories will become etched on your heart. Know that you are precisely where you are supposed to be. Study hard. Stay on the path of virtue. The rewards will come."* I learned to trust that voice, because it was telling me the truth.

As a new lawyer I worked on Wall Street, for the wonderful law firm of Cahill, Gordon & Reindel. The impeccable attorneys and firm leadership there encouraged us to take on *pro bono* public interest initiatives when we could, and I eagerly heeded that invitation. Soon, I was part of a housing court reform project and later an affordable housing initiative aimed at preventing the wholesale conversion of subsidized apartments into luxury condominiums. A team of lawyers, politicians and administrators from New York City government gathered to assess options and determine how best to accommodate the needs of the working poor families of lower Manhattan while recognizing the promise of economic revitalization for the area.

We would meet every Tuesday and often, at the close of those meetings, I would find myself feeling frustrated at the bureaucratic machinations of those in power and the snail's pace of progress. On one of those Tuesday nights I phoned home, principally to complain and to vent. My dad answered, and I began my litany of grievances: *"Daddy, the politicians aren't listening to me. Maybe it's because I'm young, or maybe because I'm a woman. Everyone seems mired in their own agenda and they aren't committed to the people behind the issues. There are real families whose futures are at stake here. Where will they live if this doesn't get resolved in their favor? But this committee doesn't care about that. This committee . . . ."*

Right there, mid-sentence, my dad interrupted me. He had heard enough and he refused to be an accomplice to my collection of grievances and perceived victimization. Instead, he said, *"Stop. You are focusing too much on what you are not getting, and not thinking enough about what you are not giving. Whatever is missing from this effort is whatever you refuse to give it. What is it that you have not yet brought to the table? You speak of the families whose lives hang in the balance. Have you met those families?"* I answered that I knew of them only on paper. He replied, *"Go and meet them. Bring your committee to meet them. Let their stories set the course for your group's work."*

"Where there is no love, put love, and you will find love."

I thought about the words: *Whatever is missing from any effort is whatever you refuse to give it.* Then I remembered the words of St. Paul, words that I had actually selected as my "favorite quote" for my high school yearbook photo: *"Where there is no love, put love, and you will find love."* Instead of infusing the task at hand with love—love for the constituencies that we were privileged to serve, love for the promise of justice, love for the humanness and humanity of the enterprise—I was infusing it with limiting judgments and ego-driven indictments. I realized then what had to be done.

Rather than dwell on what I detested—the politicization of the process—I reached out to the legal services attorneys on the committee whose example I admired. Together we organized a tenants' meeting at the building whose continued existence was threatened by the gentrification effort. We arranged to have our committee's next meeting become a part of that larger gathering of the affected tenants. There, the fear and worry of the residents, many of them parents to small children, became real. We heard from a mom who was holding down two jobs at minimum wage and still struggling to make the monthly rent, from a young man whose new job finally took him off the streets and into a place to call his own, and on it went. In those stories, we came to know the point of our work, why it mattered as much as it did and what, as the lawyers, we needed to do.

"You have some really good lawyers on your side."

At the end of that long night, as we were heading for the door, I heard a voice calling, *"Lawyer."* I turned around and saw a boy, maybe ten or eleven years old. I said, *"Hey buddy, you're up so late."* He said, *"I'm here with my mom, and she is worried. You're going to help us, right?"* I smiled and said, with as much conviction as I could muster, *"Yes. Tell your mom not to worry. You have some really good lawyers on your side. It is going to be fine."* At that, I watched as the boy exhaled. I actually saw him breathe a sigh of relief. That is the moment when I fell in love with the power and the privilege that a good education provides. That is the instant when it occurred to me that a good education put to good use could relieve suffering and give the greatest gift of all—the gift of hope.

"There can be no justice without just lawyers."

That encounter represented the moment when I went from an egocentric to a purpose-motivated life. I was not going to get sidelined or distracted by dwelling on petty slights or perceived disrespect. I was no longer a collector of grievances, looking for ways to be right about my harsh judgments of others. The enterprise at hand was not about feeding my ego. It was about the clients and constituencies whose lives hung in the balance between justice and its absence. As my colleague and civil rights champion Shavar Jeffries has said, *"There can be no justice without just lawyers."* I was determined to be a just lawyer.

That resolve is what I had been withholding from our committee's work. Now, I brought it, and I was met at that place of commitment by similar-minded champions. The resources that we needed showed up. The system started to work on our behalf. The building was saved from conversion and its tenants were safe.

No matter the context, a good education will equip you to be a giver of hope. It will allow you to be a voice for those who have yet to find their own.

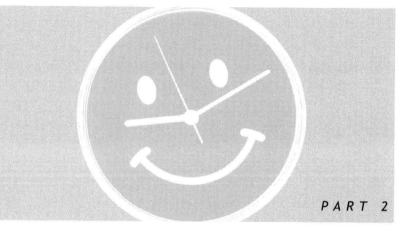

PART 2

For School, Work and Life, Five Guideposts to Live By

- *Remember who you are and where you come from. You stand on the shoulders of giants, and you vindicate their sacrifices by living the promise they foresaw.*

- *Remember Whose you are. You are never alone.*

- *Be mindful of the power of your words. Declare right now that you love school. Your life will match your level of expectation.*

- *Be of service. The surest way out of your pain is to help others out of theirs. The surest way to grow in stature is to help others to grow in theirs.*

- *Have your own answer to the question "who do you think you are?" You are a champion of the underdog, a voice for those yet to find their own, a giver of hope and a game-changer for the greater good.*

CHAPTER 5

The First Guidepost: Remember Who You Are and Where You Come From

We suffer when we forget the victories of our histories. Remember who you are and where you come from. Your parents, grandparents, their parents and ancestors before them struggled, sacrificed and overcame so that you would have the opportunity to be where you are at this very moment. The hard work has already been done. The table has been set. All you need to do is take your seat, respectfully and with great humility but also with the presence of mind to know that you belong here, you will thrive here, and you will use your life to bear living witness to the legacy of virtue that preceded you.

In school, at work and throughout life, stay close to the people who love you the most, who believe in you and who will be there to remind you of the song in your heart.

Most suffering comes when we forget the triumphs of our histories. I remember where I come from when I think about the struggles of my parents and the pain that our family endured growing up poor in Brooklyn, New York. My dad, an Italian immigrant without the benefit of a formal education, could find work only on the docks, as a longshoreman. Even working overtime, the wages made it hard to pay the bills. I remember the shame that my mom felt when the electric company turned off our power, and the dread that came when the landlord would pound on the door because the rent was late.

My parents endured the indignities felt every day by the working poor. My dad's own hopes of becoming a lawyer were squashed by the exigencies of circumstance and poverty, but he understood that education could be a great equalizer. He and my mom worked so that their four children might one day have a better life anchored in the opportunities that a professional degree could provide. My parents' calculation was correct: each of us went on to earn advanced degrees, and we now enjoy a quality of life that my parents dreamed of. As we have grown in stature, we pay it forward every day. Actually, we have grown in stature *because* we pay it forward every day.

"You are not what you are called. You are what you answer to."

As a little girl, I remember looking through my dad's union book. At the time, my dad joined the effort to unionize the workers so that conditions on the docks might be improved. That effort was met with strong resistance from management. An anti-union antagonist had scrawled some terrible ethnic slurs on my dad's book. I could not yet understand all of the words scribbled there, but I knew that they were meant to hurt my dad. I started to cry as I said, *"Dad, we have to erase these words. You have to do something. You can't let them call you that."* My dad replied, *"I know that I am not what those words try to say I am. I am not that. And I will not erase those words because I want the person who wrote them to know that the work of progress will continue not because of his actions, but in spite of them."*

Years later, one of my students sent me a photo of a wall inscribed with the words, *"You are not what you are called. You are what you answer to."* That was my dad's point.

We have the choice, every day, to decide what we will answer to. Remember that whenever someone tries to make you feel small. Turn to the people who love you the most when you need to be reminded of what you are and what you are not. Let them help you to decide what to answer to.

Today, say what needs to be said to the people you love the most.

My dad's dreams of becoming a lawyer were lived through me. By the time I was a young law professor, my dad had become a chef of some renown **(see Chapter 25 on How to Prepare Penne Vodka)**. On a humid Saturday in May, our entire family gathered for a birthday celebration. My dad prepared a feast, and as he cooked, I caught him up on the events of the week. I am the oldest of four children, and my dad reminded me to keep the youngest, my brother Louis who would soon graduate from law school, "on the right road." *"My job is done,"* he said with great pride. I protested, reminding him that he was still young and had yet to see my younger siblings get married, the birth of grandchildren and the countless milestones still to come. We changed topics as he threw in the pasta.

Later that evening, the smoke from the birthday cake's candles set off my dad's asthma. (He developed acute asthma during his time on the docks. This was before the advent of occupational safety regulations.) As a precaution, we decided to make a quick trip to the hospital to get him treatment and some relief. My mom encouraged the rest of the family to stay put. We would have the cake later.

By the time we got to the hospital, it became clear that matters had gone from bad to worse. I frantically screamed to the nurse on call, *"Please help us. My father can't breathe."* As I turned to face my dad, he whispered to me in Italian, *"Leave this one alone."* I burst into tears as I realized that he knew something, perhaps all day long, that I did not want to know. He would be leaving us on that day.

And so he did. Hours later, my mom, brother and I returned home to the cake still on the table. It was my birthday cake. It was my birthday celebration. My dad has always said that his life, the life that mattered, began the day he became a dad. Somehow, by choosing this day, the anniversary of the first day of his becoming a dad, he was telling us that his journey was completed. Even his final counsel to me, *"Leave this one alone,"* told me everything I needed to know. All my life, I was my parents' fiercest advocate and my family's champion, the lawyer-in-training and then the attorney fighting for their rights. This time, there was no argument to be made, no cause to advance.

"Leave this one alone."

It is now many years later, and still I return to those words to help me to know when to dive in and when to wait at the pier, when to take up a matter and when to let it be. On the occasion of my dad's funeral, each one of his four children took up the task of giving testimony to the life that he lived. I began with the words of Carlos Castaneda, as told in one of the Don Juan allegories. There, the elder sage turns to the younger man who is filled with the hubris and arrogance of youth and quietly says, *"The trouble with you is, you think you have time."*

The delusion that we have all the time in the world may be the trouble with all of us. The time is now to love with all of your heart. Today, at this very moment, say what needs to be said. Send a text or, better yet, write a letter of gratitude to the person or persons who have so much to do with who you are and where you come from.

This world is yours. You will grow in stature as you touch the sky. Still, tend to your roots. Let them nourish you and ground you in the bedrock of your first principles. *Remember who you are and where you come from.*

The challenge ahead transcends any of the more immediate hurdles that you will surmount. The true challenge for the years to come is to hold tight to your ideals, your goodness and your commitment to exalting the kinder virtues. When the naysayers pop up to shake your resolve, stand firm and remember that you never, ever stand alone.

All who have come before you, who believe in you and who have so much to do with your being where you are at this very moment are holding you, guiding you and lighting your road. To lose your sense of self because of defeatist ideas, or as a consequence of the assessments of others, is to disrespect that legacy. Never give up. You are more talented than you know, and the best is yet to be.

There is an ancient proverb that says, *"To get to the fruit of the tree, you must go out on a limb."* Get out there on that limb, the branch that bears the name of honor. Know that below you there will always be a safety net, composed of the arms outstretched and interlocked of all who have loved you, who respect you and who stand strong and ready to catch you if and when you sometimes fall. Those people are here for you now, whether in body or in spirit. Count on them. While they are here, love them with all your heart. When they leave this place and time, know that they carry you. Love does not die.

You stand on the shoulders of giants, and you vindicate their sacrifices by living the promise they foresaw.

CHAPTER 6

The Second Guidepost: Remember *Whose* You Are. You Are Never Alone

You do not live by yourself or solely for yourself.

You are never alone. You are a child of God, and the divinity in you is the divinity in all. Each of us is better than the worst thing we have ever done. No one is beyond the promise of redemption, and the virtue in some can be ignited in all. Let your life bear living witness to the power of transcendence.

Herman Melville was right that countless threads connect you to the brilliant tapestry of the whole of humanity. You are a citizen of the world. You belong to a community whose sum is even more magnificent than any of its parts. To serve that community you are now preparing your mind and spirit. You will be a champion of the underdog and a voice for those who have yet to find their own.

Remember that you do not live solely for yourself. What you are accomplishing now you are achieving for the countless clients and constituencies, as yet nameless and unknown, who will be counting on you to make the difference that only you can make. You will be their giver of hope.

Trust that *"there is a star that you are under, put there for a reason."* You are precisely where you are meant to be, and this is a compassionate world. It is rooting for you every step of the way. There is a force that meets good with good.

In school, at work and in life, the most important question is not *what* you want to be, but *who* you want to be.

Take some time now to arrive at your set of first principles— the virtues that inform the person you want to be. How do you want to be thought of? What do you want said about you? The characteristics that you want to embrace should include generosity, kindness, compassion, honesty and the commitment to excellence. Let your first principles be guided by the recognition that you are in the world but not *of* it. Your source transcends the limitations of this place and time and it is vast, loving and beneficent. It does not test us. It cheers for us.

To stay within your circle of first principles, commit to the practice of relentless gratitude.

Be the most grateful person in every room. Look for the nobility in all people and in all things. Recognize that this moment will never be here again. Say what needs to be said in the pursuit of unyielding appreciation.

Ask to be used for a purpose mightier than yourself.

If you send up only one prayer every day, make that prayer *"Use me."* Those two words demonstrate your willingness to be a vessel through which good and noble work can be done. They will help you to stay on purpose, and they will assure that you are always found where you need to be.

Divine guidance responds to the slightest whisper, whether in the form of *"use me"* or *"help me."* Not too long ago and far from home, I was lost on my way to a concert. A young woman appeared out of nowhere and had the compassion to say, *"You seem lost. May I help you?"* I explained where I needed to be, and she was kind enough to reply, *"That's hard to find from here. I will walk you over to the concert hall."* As we walked, and without knowing anything about me, she told me that she was finishing her undergraduate studies and that her dream was to go to law school. She was the first person in her family to pursue that ambition, and she was hoping to find a mentor. I told her that she just had. She is now my mentee, and just as she graced my path, I can now grace hers. On that occasion, both she and I were found where we needed to be.

Practice forgiveness.

Sometimes people will hurt you, whether unintentionally or, worse, on purpose. Forgive them. Be informed by their actions but by no means diminished by them. That means that you will be smart enough to protect yourself from further trespass and wise enough to know that while the transgressor's actions speak volumes about him or her, they do not speak for you.

People can be cruel and reckless. You will forgive for your sake. You will forgive because you refuse to be weighed down by the boulder of resentment. You will forgive because you value yourself enough to stop hurting yourself because of what someone else did.

CHAPTER 7

The Third Guidepost: Be Mindful of the Power of Your Words

Your life will move in the direction of your most dominant rhetoric about it.

Choose your words carefully. Let what you say facilitate the cause of peace and understanding. Speak only good things about people, even when they have not yet caught up to your level of expectation for them. They will. Centuries ago, the German philosopher Goethe got it right when he observed, *"If you treat an individual as he is, he will remain how he is. But if you treat him as if he were what he ought to be and could be, he will become what he ought to be and could be."*

Stop saying mean things about yourself.

Speak only good things about yourself. Be disciplined with your self-talk. Do not be your worst critic. When you look in the mirror, what are you saying to yourself? When you make a mistake, how badly do you berate yourself? Would you ever think of being

39

that unkind to another? Show yourself the same generosity that you so readily extend to others.

Rather than listen to your inner monologue, talk *to* yourself. Be your own cheerleader and your own coach. For guidance on what your self-talk should sound like, imagine that a six year old child is always following you, watching your every move and listening to your every thought. Suppose that everything that she will come to know about the world and her place in it will come from what she hears from you. What would you want her to hear and to believe? **Be that.**

You are enough.

Stop holding yourself to some external model of perfection. It is an illusion. When you begin to be unkind to yourself, imagine that very innocent child standing beside you, bearing silent witness to your self-directed brutality and internalizing it. Is that what you want to teach? When the voices of doubt creep in—*"You can't do this," "You're not that smart," "You're ugly," "You're fat"*—interrupt them in their tracks and declare firmly, *"I am enough."*

You do not have to be perfect, or anything close to the distorted standard that the "smart police" or "beauty police" would have you internalize. All of that is sleight of hand and digitized fakery.

The two questions to ask at the end of each day.

At the end of each day, ask yourself two questions. *First, did you try your best?* If you got into the ring, no matter that you might have gotten clobbered once there, it was a good day. Tomorrow, with a fresh start, you will enter once again, stronger and wiser. Getting knocked down is not what counts. *What matters is getting back up.*

Second, did you bring love into the world? If you brought a smile to someone's face, made another's load lighter, sowed seeds of kindness or stirred the pot of compassion, then no matter what you think you looked like or sounded like, regardless of the number on the scale and irrespective of anyone else's critique, *you were beautiful.*

Declare right now that you love school and that you love any job that you are lucky enough to have.

You might be thinking, *"But I haven't started school yet,"* or *"But I'm not sure yet if I like it,"* or, *"I hate my job."* None of that matters.

Hear me now and believe me later: **Your life will meet you at your level of expectation for it.** What that means is, even if you have to fake it until you make it, you should begin, right now, to enthusiastically declare your passion and admiration for everything about the education that you are (or are about to) receive and the job that you are doing. *"Where there is no love put love, and you shall find love."*

Starting now, relentlessly extend gratitude to every single person on your path.

In school and at work, say thank you on a daily basis to everyone whose efforts contribute to your day, from the security guard at the front desk to the cashier in the cafeteria to the classmate seated next to you to the teacher instructing you to the co-worker in the next cubicle to the janitor emptying the wastebaskets to the stranger who will soon be your friend.

Be the most interested and grateful person in every room. Think about what a child does when you give him a really great gift. As he jumps up and down for joy, what are you thinking? Maybe, *"I love this child. And I want to give him more!"* Be that child. Your immense gratitude for the good in your life will bring you even greater good.

The people that you meet will rise to your level of expectation for them.

Prepare to love your classmates, teachers and colleagues. That preparation has very little to do with them, and everything to do with you. Your experiences will rise (or fall) to your level of expectation. Your life will take you in the path of your predominant thoughts and words about it.

Whenever you think a good or positive thought about another, say it out loud.

We tend to find it easier to criticize than to praise. That may be a conditioned response, or simply a way to avoid our vulnerability. Sometimes we decline to tell people the positive things we think and feel about them for fear of being thought a phony or a fake. But trust me on this: our lizard brains—even the most primitive parts of our cerebral functions—can spot authenticity a mile away. We know sincerity. When you say what you mean, truthfully and with kindness, you will not be misunderstood.

If you think that a classmate made an excellent point in class, tell her. If you admire the statesmanship of a student leader on campus, tell him. If you strive to emulate the example of a particularly generous friend, tell her. If a colleague or supervisor inspires you, say so. If you are on the bus and you notice that the driver greets every passenger with courtesy and respect, compliment the driver. If a salesperson is doing a great job under pressure, say so. There is so much that is negative and toxic out there in the marketplace of ideas. Do not leave the high-minded and positive observations unsaid.

When you seek out the good in others, and then proclaim that good to them and about them, you bring good to yourself. There is a Chinese proverb that states, *"A bit of fragrance always clings to the hand that gives you flowers."* What you do for others, you do for yourself. What you do *to* others, you do to yourself. Take care then in all that you put out into the world, for it cannot help but return to you.

Sometimes, no matter that you have professed your love for school or your job, it will feel as though neither loves you back.

It takes courage to decide to love school, your classmates, your teachers, colleagues and friends. To love is to risk disappointment. But choose love anyway. Sometimes life will break your heart. But it can never break your spirit. There is a sacred, inviolate and untouchable part of you that cannot be reached by the indignities of the world. It will allow you to transcend all injustice and rise up from the ashes wiser and even more compassionate, because a heart that sometimes breaks has more room.

Some days will be harder than others. Especially then, emerge from the rubble of a bad grade, a letter of rejection, a dismal encounter or a failed relationship and stand even taller than you did before. It did not kill you. It is making you stronger. Dig in your heels, become the stubborn person that you know you can be, and declare, *"The best is yet to be!"*

Greatness will be yours *not* because you never failed. Greatness will be yours because sometimes you did fail, *but still you persisted.*

You will succeed because even In the face of all disenchantment you remained anchored in your firm conviction that *the best is yet to come*. Refusing to join the chorus of cynics, you stuck with the choir of angels. And with that choice, you changed the world for the better.

The Fourth Guidepost:
Be of Service

The surest way to allay your own pain is to help others find ways out of theirs.

Decide now that wherever your path takes you, you will use your expertise to ease the suffering of others. Keep that as your aim, and the opportunities to serve will find you.

There is much to be done. Too many are denied access to the basic necessities of life. Heed the call to service, no matter the cynic's chides. Cynicism hardens hearts and complacency numbs the generous impulse. In the midst of rising seas of need, you will choose to do what you can with the time that you have. And that will make all the difference.

Look for the starfish now in your hands.

There is a parable of a child on the beach. The tide precipitously pulls out, leaving thousands of starfish stranded on the shore. If not thrown back, they will dry up and die. The boy begins picking them up, one at a time, and casting them back to sea. A passerby sees this and says, *"There are too many of them left here. What you're doing doesn't matter."* The boy looks down at the starfish in his hand—the starfish whose life he is about to spare—and replies, *"But it does matter to this starfish."*

Every act of generosity matters. There will be many starfish on your journey. Seek the wisdom to see what needs to be seen and the courage to respond with big-heartedness. Vow to share your emerging bounty of influence. There are many people, most still unknown to you, who have been waiting for you to earn this degree so that you can change their lives for the better. You will not let them down.

Listen to your mother.

My mom, Mary, has the biggest heart on the planet. She lives in Brooklyn and works in lower Manhattan. Invariably, whether she is talking with her neighbors or overhearing others' conversations, she learns of people's struggles. It might be a woman worried because she received an eviction notice, a student new to the area who cannot find an affordable place to live, a parent worried about her child's learning difficulties or an employee who is being treated unfairly. Irrespective, my mom will approach the individual, whether friend or stranger, and indicate that one of her four children will be able to help with their troubles. My mom knows that because each of her children received the benefits of a good education.

My mom might say to the aggrieved tenant, *"My daughter Paula is an attorney and a law professor. She will help you,"* and to the worried parent, *"My daughter Rosalie is a leading expert on learning differences. She will help you,"* and to the student seeking a place to live, *"My daughter Marianne is a therapist and acclaimed educator affiliated with New York University and she can help you,"* and to the victimized employee, *"My son Louis and daughter-in-law Diane are prominent labor/employment lawyers. They will help you."* My mom then gives out our contact information.

It has always been understood that the work that my mom volunteers us for will be done free of charge. We do not balk at her requests of us, because we are our mother's children. She taught us early on to use whatever influence, opportunity and goodwill that we have for the betterment of others. She and my dad understood that a good education would be a door opener, and that it was important that we hold that door open for others.

Throughout my career, I have received countless phone calls as a result of my mom's generosity. Sometimes they come at the most inconvenient times. Sometimes I want to yell at my mother. But I always say yes. Yes, I will help you, or yes, I will find the right person to help you, and yes, I promise to follow up and no, I won't forget. I have been privileged to have spearheaded some significant legislative and policy reform throughout my career, but my most meaningful work has come because my mom taught me to see the starfish.

See what needs to be seen and respond with compassion.

On your way to and from school every day, notice the people who come into your path. Is there a homeless man at the train station? Is there a woman at the crosswalk who seems very sad? Is there a classmate or colleague on his way to the parking garage who looks like he has had a really hard day? Snap out of your own preoccupations, turn off your phone and see what needs to be seen. Do what you can, with whatever resources you have, to make the day better for that person.

Decide every day that you are going to make someone's day.

Set as your intention: *"I am going to make someone's day today."* Equip yourself to be able to do just that. Keep an extra sandwich in your backpack to give to a person who seems hungry. Carry in your pocket a $5.00 gift card to McDonald's or Dunkin' Donuts or some other local eatery and give it to someone who could really use it. Initiate a conversation with the person who seems distressed and brighten his or her mood. Sometimes all it takes is a kind word of encouragement to take a person from blue to better.

For your birthday and on special occasions, when family and friends ask what you would like, ask for bunches of $5.00 gift cards and explain why. That will inspire others to follow your example, and like a pebble in a stream, the ripples of your kindness will spread.

I began that practice in college. Still today, I carry gift cards, small bills and some food wherever I go. The week before Thanksgiving, I keep with me more substantial gift cards to supermarkets and as I perceive need, I give them away. At Christmastime, I bring wrapped toys to school and dispatch my students to find worthy recipients. They are my accomplices and I am theirs in the joy-spreading scheme.

When you ask to be used for a purpose bigger than yourself, you will be heard and your request will be answered. Keep showing up, pay attention and the opportunities will appear.

When you decide that you are going to use this day to be a giver of hope, you become a game-changer. With one generous impulse rendered one day at a time, you become a paradigm-shifter. *Your goodness will shake people out of their cynicism and despair and make them question whether they are right about their harsh judgments of the world. When they try to convict humanity, you will be their basis for reasonable doubt.*

Most of all, your assiduous commitment to the good of others will make your life beautiful. *You will be a midwife to the birth of hope.* I have had the privilege to watch as hope has sprung from the most desolate places. My life has never been the same.

Super Bowl Sunday.

Several years ago, on Super Bowl Sunday, I stood at the express checkout line of our local supermarket behind a dad and his young daughter. The little girl was about 6 years old, and the dad looked worn down. Their cart was small and contained only essentials—milk, eggs, bread—and one indulgence, a festive little cake shaped like a football and brightly decorated. The dad was very carefully watching the screen as his items were rung, and it became clear that he needed to be sure that he had enough in cash and food assistance coupons to be able to pay for the transaction. When it came time to ring up the cake, the dad realized that he was out of funds. He set the cake off to the side and told the cashier that he would not be purchasing it. I watched the little girl's face, and my heart broke.

I had to do something, but I did not want to embarrass or humiliate the man. I had a twenty dollar bill in my hand to pay for my items. I quietly let that $20 fall to the ground. Then, I tapped the man on the shoulder and asked, *"Did you drop that?"* He looked down and said, *"No, that's not mine."* I picked up the bill and insisted, *"No, I think you dropped this. It's not mine, and I thought I saw it fall from your pocket."* Our eyes locked, and in that instant he realized what I was doing. With grace and a nod of gratitude, he took the bill, and asked the cashier to add the cake to his order. The little girl hugged her dad and then practically hugged the cake.

In the years since that day, I have never again seen that man. But I carry him and his daughter in my heart. They are there whenever I begin to wonder if what we do matters. I can hear them whisper, *"It does."*

As you learn, teach others.

In school and at work, you will be learning so much. Share your newfound knowledge. Go back to your local high school, middle school or grade school and meet with the principal. Indicate your willingness to give a talk, to be a mentor and to help with those parts of the curriculum that you are best at. I teach *Loving the Law*, an elective class, to middle school children in my hometown. I deputize the class to be "agents of positive change." I teach about good citizenship and the promise of our living Constitution. Guest speakers, experts in their fields, visit us each week to teach about family law, finance, criminal procedure, personal injury law, negotiation, employment law, animal welfare law and more.

The best way to learn something is to teach it. You will grow in expertise as you summon the courage to get out there and share your emerging repertoire of knowledge with the world.

CHAPTER 9

The Fifth Guidepost: Have Your Own Answer to the Question: *Who Do You Think You Are?*

When you decide to be a person of principle, invariably others will ask, "*Who do you think you are?*" Have your own answer to that question. Do not let the world answer for you.

Go back to your circle of first principles. *That is who you think you are.* You are a child of God and a citizen of the world. You belong to a community greater than yourself. You are a person of integrity. You are a champion of the underdog, a crusader for justice and a voice for those who have yet to find their own. Most of all, you are a giver of hope.

With time, the world will stop testing your perception of yourself. It will realize that it can take you at your word and because your word is good it will cheer you on. It will greet your generous impulse with a sigh of relief.

Your experiences will mirror back to you the intentions behind your actions.

Let what you do be consistent with who you think you are. Be clear about your intentions before you act. Intend to be an agent for positive change. Intend to heal the pain of others. Intend to proclaim the virtuous. An intention must always return to its source. You will reap the consequences of your intentions.

You are a champion of the underdog.

My son Michael played basketball in school. In the sixth grade, he came home from a game dejected. He told me that the other team lost, but not because they were outplayed. They lost because more than half of the team did not have suitable footwear or athletic attire. Michael noticed this during play, as some of the boys were tripping and skidding on the court. Their sneakers were frayed, without laces or adequate soles.

My son was dismayed at the injustice of it all. How could it be that the kids did not have basketball shoes? I explained that those shoes are expensive and maybe their families just couldn't afford them. *"What can we do?"* he asked. I answered that he had already done half the work. He had chosen to see what needed to be seen. Now, together we could be part of the solution.

We decided to start a sneaker fund. The next day I mentioned the effort to my class, and with characteristic generosity my students rose to the occasion. Bake sales were held and donations solicited. Without being asked, my son contributed some of his birthday money. Soon, we had more than we imagined. I called the school's principal with the good news. She was overjoyed. She put me in touch with the Athletic Director. He couldn't believe it. With the donation, he was able to outfit each player and buy uniforms for the team. He sent us a picture of the team in their beautiful green and gold uniforms with a note that my son keeps on his bulletin board to this day.

You are a voice for those who have yet to find their own.

My children will not abide meanness. A new boy joined my son's seventh grade class, and as a newcomer he had a hard time fitting in. Seizing on his vulnerability, some of the other students began making fun of him and excluding him from recess activities. My son saw this, and did not like it. He described how, during the daily football game, that boy sat alone on the school steps. Apparently some of the other players had made plain that they did not want the new kid slowing down the game. Michael took a stand, and said, *"If he doesn't play, I don't play."* Michael walked off the field, and sat with the new boy. They talked and Michael learned that the boy was learning how to weld, and that he could create art from melted metal. He could even take some of the objects that he made and, with his mom, create greeting cards.

Michael and his new friend continued their recess talks until one day the invitation was extended for both of them to join the game. Mike said to his buddy, *"If you're in, I'm in."* Together they played, and soon the new boy was part of the crew.

Later that year, Michael wanted to celebrate his birthday with a sleepover at our house. He invited every boy in the class. The party was a big success, and at the end of the night I went downstairs to check on everyone. All of the boys were asleep, except for the new boy. He was sitting up, simply looking around the room. I asked him if everything was ok, if he needed anything or if he was homesick. He replied, *"No, it's not that. I'm just happy. I'm trying not to fall asleep because I want to remember this day."*

The next week a card arrived in the mail, addressed to our family. It was from the new boy and his family. The card featured a beautiful piece of art that the boy had welded. At the top were the words, *"No act of kindness is ever wasted."*

PART 3

Preparing to Be Happy in School, at Work and in Relationships

Commit to the practices outlined in this section to be your best in school, at work and in relationships. Check in with its pages often. They will provide a safe harbor in sometimes stormy seas.

CHAPTER 10

Arrive At Your Set of First Principles

You want to be a person of integrity.

It is important that you take some time now to think about the virtues and values that matter most to you. Those are your first principles, meaning the code that you live by. They are the moral compass by which you chart your course and comport your behavior.

When your words and actions are in accord with your first principles, your life will run smoothly. When what you say and what you do departs from your first principles, you will veer off course. When that happens, as it sometimes will, the quickest way to get back on track is to remind yourself that you are a person of integrity and that you will make the adjustments and the amends that a person of integrity would make to get back to good.

Decide now what you stand for. What is the highest and best expression of you? How would you want to be remembered? What will your legacy be? What are you willing to enter the room for? What are you willing to walk out for?

Think of your first principles as a circle. When your behavior keeps you within the circle, you are in the flow and you feel good. When your actions are outside the circle, you feel guilt, that nagging tug at your conscience. That is your signal to get back in the circle.

No matter that you will sometimes stray from it, always return to your center of virtue. Do this for the sake of others, and for your own sake. In a world of infinite possibilities, you will not get what you want. *You will get what you are.* The law of reciprocity is always at work. We get what we give. We are denied what we withhold. Give what you want to receive.

Be clear about your first principles. Write them down. Refer to them often. They will be your safe harbor against the changing winds of time.

Finish these sentences *"These are the central values on which I base my life: _____" "These are the attributes I admire most: _____" "This is how I hope others would describe me: _____"* Write down the answers on an index card. Use that card as a bookmark when you begin school or a new job, or start a new relationship. Refer to it often. It will help you to keep your head on straight, especially when others seem to be losing theirs. We suffer when we stray from our first principles. We find relief when we return to them.

I did that exercise before I began law school. I jotted down the answers on an index card, and I kept that card on my bulletin board, where I would see it every day. On that card here is what I wrote:

"I value intelligence and I respect kindness even more. I stand for the realization of equal access to justice for all. I believe in the promise of redemption and the

power of love. I admire the relentless commitment to excellence when it is practiced with compassion. I seek to emulate those who stay above the fray and whose high-mindedness has no room for the petty or mean spirited. I want to be remembered for seeing the good in everyone, because it is there."

Everything that you say and do begins with an intention. Keep your intentions consistent with your first principles. That way, you assure not only your success, but also your substance.

Integrity is when the outside matches the inside. You live a life of substance when your words and actions are virtue made visible.

Integrity is present when you talk the talk *and* walk the walk. You live a life of integrity when you speak the truth compassionately rather than brutally. There is too much brutality in the world already. You lead with integrity when you say what you mean and mean what you say. You practice integrity when you are able to integrate the pursuit of excellence with the steadfast commitment to decency.

You demonstrate integrity when you respect intelligence, but respect kindness more. To separate virtue from your professional pursuits is to risk losing your soul. To segment off whole aspects of yourself to become something you think you are supposed to be is to lose your integrity.

You live with integrity when you bring all of you—artist, scholar, musician, teacher, student, parent, scientist, lover of literature, athlete, chef and the list goes on—to your endeavors. You contain multitudes. Let other see the brilliance of your many facets. The very word *"integrity"* comes from the Latin *integritas,* meaning wholeness. To integrate all that you are into all that you do is to lead with integrity.

There is no room for duplicity or phoniness in a life lived with integrity. There is an absence of honor whenever you say something *to* a person but something quite different *about* that person. You will feel the consequences of any duality or inauthenticity that you participate in. Your conscience will bother you and you will feel like a fraud. That feeling will diminish your power in the world and erode your sense of self. Hence, for your own sake as well as for the sake of all others, declare right now that you will live a life of integrity.

We all hope that the people we look up to *are really like that*. One of my students once told the class of the time that she was in the audience of the Oprah Winfrey show. The first question the class asked was, *"What is she really like?"* (She is wonderful.) Our higher instincts are vindicated when we are able to validate that the generosity or valor that we perceive to be present in another is indeed there. Our lesser instincts are fed by the tabloids, blogs, virtual thugs and gossip-mongers whose aim is to convince us otherwise.

Stay away from the bottom-feeders and traffickers in human frailties. Stay above the fray.

When someone starts to gossip, you have several high-minded options. First, simply walk away. Extricate yourself from the conversation. Second, say to the person, *"You are better than that. We all are."* Then, change the topic. Third, help to correct the speaker's perceptions. That is the most powerful way to respond. If you know the person that is the target of the hurtful speech, speak about the goodness and virtue that you know she possesses. If you do not know the person well or at all or if it has been difficult for you to arrive at a positive estimation of her, be the voice of compassion by simply stating that as she lives and learns she will do better.

When using the internet, do not let the anonymity of a comments section entice you to write something that is simply not worthy of you. Use social media responsibly. **(See Chapter 13: How to Use Social Media Responsibly)**. Let your digitized imprint be principled, generous and positive. Proclaim what you are *for* instead of decrying what you are ***against***. If you read a post that is mean-spirited, privately message its author to indicate how and why you think he or she ought to be self-corrective.

Live your life so that those who know you best see your best.

Recently, an esteemed judge counseled our law students to *"love your work and work at your love."* While in school, do not neglect the people who matter most to you. Tend to your most precious relationships. Show up for the people you love, and let them see not just the stressed you but the best of you.

At social occasions, my children are often asked by my students and colleagues, *"Is she really this nice at home?"* One of my greatest moments came when I overheard my daughter reply, *"No. She's actually nicer."* Live your life so that the person you are at home is even more generous than the person the world sees.

Your life will move in the direction of greatness when what you say and what you do is reliably consistent with who you want to be.

You will grow in power and stature as your daily habits comport with your first principles. Strive each day to keep your words and actions within your circle of core values. When you find yourself acting outside the circle, be self-corrective. Apologize, make amends and forgive yourself. Make the adjustments that you need to make to get back to center and then move forward. Stop re-living the incident that took you off track. Stop *"should-ing"* on yourself, as in *"I should have done this"* or *"I shouldn't have done that."* You are human, and if you had nothing left to learn you would be dead.

Do not live a neutral life. Decide what you stand for.

Take a stand for decency, fairness and the cause of justice. Stand on the side of virtue. Stick up for the underdog. Be a voice for someone who has yet to find his own. In the presence of cruelty, do not be impartial. There is a well of courage inside of you that you have not even begun to tap. Go to that well and draw from it. Call out meanness and wrongdoing. Speak your peace truthfully and with dignity, *but speak your peace.* To remain neutral in the presence of injustice is to stand for nothing. Complacency is the enemy of the good.

Call out bullying for what it is—cowardice disguised as force.

Defy the push of the crowds and take a stand for justness. If you see someone being victimized by another's wrongdoing, say something. Get in the way of the bully's brand of brutality by interrupting it in its tracks. Bullying is weakness disguised as force.

Decide that you will be a leader, not a follower. Do not allow your association with anyone or anything to cause you to become complicit in the hurting of another. Do not allow your association with anyone or anything to cause you to become complicit in the hurting of yourself.

Speak passionately about what you stand for, rather than what you stand *against.*

What you resist persists. Let your life be directed by what you admire, rather than what repulses you. When Mother Teresa was asked to attend anti-war rallies, she always declined. *"Ask me to attend a pro-peace rally,"* she would reply, *"and I will be there."* The great game-changers of history knew that we grow in power and stature when we decide to firmly stand *for* something, rather than *against* something else.

CHAPTER 11

How to Stay within Your Circle of First Principles

To stay within your circle of first principles, habituate three techniques: *1.) say thank you countless times a day, 2.) be of service in all settings and 3.) forgive generously.*

Say thank you countless times a day.

A heart that is grateful does not have room for meanness or pettiness. Say thank you when you see a thing of beauty. Say thank you when you observe an act of kindness. Even say thank you when you observe someone behaving badly because you are grateful to know what not to do.

One afternoon, as I was leaving the law school's parking lot, I stopped to ask the attendant, Bernadette, how she was. She replied, *"I am blessed to be in the day."* That is a perfect statement and a perfect response. No matter how the day is going, **YOU ARE LUCKY ENOUGH TO BE IN IT.**

You are still here. That means that you have another chance to make new choices. If the day is bad because you argued with someone, reach out and apologize, even if it was not your fault. You can be right or you can be happy. Choose happiness. Then say thank you because you took the high road.

If the day is less than great because you are tired, find the time to take a nap. Make that a priority. Do not underestimate the need for rest. Then say thank you because you found a place to rest.

If the day is hard because you are simply not at your best, know that everyone has off days and let it go. Then say thank you because you are privileged to be in school and tomorrow is going to be a better day.

Whenever things start to go wrong, stop the trajectory of doom in its tracks and declare firmly, *"No! This is not how the day is going to go."* Then immediately shift your focus from whatever just went wrong to everything that is going right. Step away from the computer screen and find someone to hug. Send flowers to make someone's day. Put on *Pharrell* and dance with your dog. If you are stuck in traffic, begin praying for the drivers to your left and to your right. Your day will move in the direction of your focal point. Focus on the good in your midst and the good to come.

Be of service in all settings.

Make every context in which you find yourself less about you and more about how you can be of service. Seek out ways to help. At the start of each day, declare that your intention is to make another's load lighter. Leave your ego at the door of every room that you are about to enter, and generously do something so that the room is better because you were there. That might mean adding clarity where there was confusion, speaking kind words, baking for someone, mopping the floor or making someone laugh. No matter the form that it takes, be of service.

Generously forgive.

Do not be a collector of grievances. They will only clutter your closet. Give everyone the benefit of the doubt, and stay above the fray. Let go of your resentments. There is a Native American wisdom that *"it is not the miles ahead that wear us out. It is the grain of sand in our shoe."* Do not let another's transgression wear you down. Shake out your shoe and keep moving forward.

We stray from our core values when we seek revenge or when we decide that we need to tell anyone who will listen about the misdeed that has us so agitated. When someone hurts your feelings, take it up with him or her and no one else. Do not enlist the sympathy of others and do not give the matter a life of its own by spreading it around. That sort of behavior will reflect poorly on you, and it may burn bridges best left intact.

"No tree has branches so foolish as to fight among themselves." (Ojibwa Indian Wisdom)

Do not fight with your family members. Be at peace with your friends. For that matter, endeavor to construe family broadly. Generously construe your version of *"us"* so that *"us"* versus *"them"* conceptualizations yield to the essential truth that we all cry the same tears.

CHAPTER 12

Ten Ways to Make Wise Choices

In school, at work and in life, you will be the sum total of the choices you make. This chapter contains a set of do's and don'ts to help you to make wise choices.

1) Choose your friends carefully.

To *know a person, meet their friends.* That means that people will make assumptions about you based on who you study with, who you socialize with and who you are closest to. Surround yourself with friends, classmates and colleagues who share your first principles, believe in the importance of living with integrity and care about their futures. Study with people who are serious about doing well in school. Socialize with people who are generous, kind and understand the consequences of stupidity. Avoid the "cool" group, however that is defined in your given context, the reckless rebels, the dismissive elitists and the pockets of meanness. It is ok to be a nerd and, later on, to marry a nerd. Nerds tend to rule the world.

2) Leave any relationship that makes you feel small, demeaned or denigrated.

Abuse only escalates over time. If you are with someone who calls you names, get out of the relationship. If you are with someone who is jealous of your success, get out. If you are with someone who tries to keep you from your family and friends, get out. If you are with someone who tries to control you, get out. If you are with someone who hits you, even once, get out. It is never only once. No matter the tears and apologies, get out and do not look back. Love yourself enough to set healthy boundaries. You are no one's punching bag (figuratively or, God forbid, literally). You are a person of goodness and substance and you deserve to be treated that way. *Treat yourself that way, and trust that the world will come to follow your example. You will meet your match.*

3) Study hard and work hard.

When studying, turn off your cell phone, use your computer only for studying or work purposes, and do what needs to be done. The child inside of you will try to get you to take frequent breaks or find things to do that are more fun than the work at hand. Have a talk with the child that still dwells inside you and say, *"Listen, we have to study for the next two hours. But after that, we will watch a movie"* (or play a video game, go shopping, eat ice cream, take a walk or whatever else you know would delight you.) Then, be sure to keep your word. If you do, you will observe amazing results as your inner six year old frees you to get done what needs to be done, in anticipation of the reward at the end of the task. You will instantly feel more energized and focused.

4) Drink alcohol only in moderation, and do not drink at all until you are of legal age.

This will be a difficult mandate to abide, but do it anyway. Do not come to rely on alcohol as a way to be less socially awkward or as a means of fitting in. If your friends insist that you join them in checking out of their lives by drinking, find new friends. If that seems too drastic a response, then muster the courage to say no. Eventually, friends worth having will respect your choice. Drinking underage is a crime. It also subjects you to physiological consequences that your body is not prepared for. Your brain's discernment centers are not fully developed until you reach your twenties. Drinking before then puts you at higher risk of addiction. It lowers your inhibitions, setting you up to make irresponsible and potentially irreparable choices. Don't do it.

5) Do not get a fake ID.

In high school and especially in college, it might seem like a good idea to get a phony piece of identification to demonstrate that you are 21 when you are not. That would be a poor choice to make for many reasons. Most essentially, it is a crime, punishable as a felony that can carry with it jail time. Using fake identification subjects you to charges of forgery, assuming a false identity, tampering with a public record and criminal impersonation. That criminal record stays with you for the rest of your life, and has the potential to destroy your future. As a lawyer and law professor, I have had to help my students undo the consequences of their being charged with possession of a falsified identification, and that task can be a nightmare.

6) Never drink and drive.

Having even one drink on an empty stomach could set you up for a driving under the influence charge. That charge has serious consequences and it creates a permanent record subject to disclosure for the rest of your life. It has to be disclosed on school applications and job applications. It will stigmatize you and haunt you. Never get behind the wheel if you have had a drink.

7) Never get into a car where the driver has been drinking.

Your life will be at risk. Others' lives will be at risk. Moreover, anyone reckless enough to get behind the wheel when cognitively impaired has bad judgment, and that poor judgment no doubt spills over into other aspects of that person's life. You do not want to be friends with a train wreck. You do not want to be in a vehicle that gets stopped, only to be searched with that search yielding contraband. No matter your innocence, you will be brought into the police precinct and you may find yourself held under the heading of "guilt by association."

8) Never text and drive.

The temptation to do so is great, particularly at a red light or on a vast, empty expanse of road where the risk seems small. Resist that temptation, because when you are behind the wheel, no risk is small. *When you get in the car, put your phone out of reach.* It can wait. Countless tragedies have occurred because too many drivers succumbed to the illusion that they could send out a quick text while keeping their eyes on the road. That is a physiological impossibility. It could kill you and it could kill someone else. If you live and you did harm because you were texting and driving, you will go to jail. In a growing number of states, criminal liability can also attach to a person who knowingly texts someone who is driving.

9) Do not post inappropriate words or photos on your social media sites.

Your digital imprint will be scrutinized by university admissions officers, prospective employers, colleagues, co-workers and actual as well as potential love interests and their families and friends. Keep what you say high-minded. Avoid overexposure in the photos that you post. Aim to be a class act. What you share online can and will reach lots of unintended recipients and some creepy viewers. Be discrete and be modest about what you choose to share.

10) Take care in what you choose to watch, read and listen to.

Avoid brutality in all its forms. Its images are haunting and have the potential over time to skew your perspective and desensitize you to the suffering of others. Retain your capacity to be shocked and appalled, so that you can respond with the power of your convictions and, when it is appropriate, the force of rightful outrage.

CHAPTER 13

How to Use Social Media Responsibly

Clean up your social media accounts.

Right now, go through your Facebook, Twitter, Instagram, Snap chat and Tumblr accounts and delete any photographs, posts or other communications that would place you in a bad light. Revisit the internet addresses that you have ascribed to your on-line accounts. Make sure that they are professional.

Admissions officers, prospective employers, current employers, co-workers and countless others will be checking your virtual footprint before making decisions that could affect your life. You do not want any inappropriate or unseemly depictions attached to your name. In these new media times of ever-intersecting circles of influence and exchange, the personal cannot help but inform the professional. Take charge of the impression that your digitized patterns create.

Keep every communication to your teachers, professors, classmates, employers, co-workers and colleagues professional and high-minded. Never hit *send* in anger.

Expect that every electronic submission that you send can and often will be forwarded to others, including unintended recipients. When you communicate with a professor, employer or co-worker by e-mail or text, keep the tone immensely respectful and professional. Do not reduce to a written form what is best said in person. Do not text or email what you can say orally. Everything that you reduce to writing, no matter the medium, creates a permanent record. It is discoverable in litigation and could come back to haunt you.

In school, if you have to miss a class, write in advance, explain and apologize. If you were in class and missed the attendance sheet, write to apologize and ask if the record can be amended to include note of your presence. If you are confused about some part of the subject matter, say so clearly but also with humility and deference. For example, state, *"I am so sorry to bother you with this, but I am having the hardest time understanding Bentham's utilitarian thesis. Here is what I think the readings get to: _____. Am I correct in that understanding?"* Another example, *"I have read and re-read the assigned materials, but I am still struggling with the problem sets. I would so much appreciate the opportunity to meet with you this week. Would that be possible?"*

Avoid colloquialisms and an informal tone. Do not place the burden of your confusion on your teacher when you write asking for help or clarification. For example, do not write, *"For the life of me I just don't get what we did in class today. Maybe you could explain it again in class tomorrow?"* Instead, try, *"As I review my notes, there are a few points that I'm afraid I don't have down yet. Would it be ok if I came by office hours later this week?"*

If you are writing to another to vent or complain, don't.

Anticipate that every one of your electronic communications can and will be shared with others. If there is a problem that must be addressed in writing, keep your tone dispassionate and professional. Know that electronic communication leaves little room for the reader to discern nuance or tone. Do not try to be funny in your correspondence. Do not try to be sarcastic or caustic. It will not work, and most likely will backfire. Avoid derisive predicates such as, *"What in the world?" "How could you possibly?" or "What were you thinking?"*

CHAPTER 14

However You Characterize School, Your Work and the People in Your Life, You Will Be Right

Whether you love or detest school, your job and the people in your life, you will be right. Life will meet you at your level of expectation. Expect great things.

Twenty years ago, anticipating the birth of our son Michael, we made plans to move from Manhattan to Cedar Grove, a small town that we did not know much about and that our friends and family had never heard of. When people asked, *"How do you feel about the move?"* I set aside all trepidation and replied, *"I am thrilled. I love our new neighborhood. I love the people who live there."* It did not matter that I had not yet met our neighbors. I was prepared to love them, not look for their faults. Sure enough, two decades later, we are still in the same house, we love our community and we are thankful for our neighbors. Still today, as new neighbors move in and friends ask, *"How are they?"* I reply, irrespective of whether I have yet met them, *"My new neighbors are wonderful. You will love them when you meet them."* Invariably, I am right.

Recently my twelve year old nephew Louie was sitting in our kitchen and asking if I happened to know anything about a new faculty member who was joining his school. *"Yes,"* I answered, *"She is fantastic. Make sure that you introduce yourself to her because she will be a great resource to you and you will learn so much from her."* Louie asked, *"When did you meet her?"* When I replied, *"I haven't yet,"* his quizzical look was answered by his mom, my sister-in-law Diane, who said, *"Louie, you just learned the Aunt Paula way."*

Give everyone and everything the benefit of the doubt.

The good in some happens to be the good in all. Sometimes people have not yet shown you their best. Be patient. Give everyone the benefit of the doubt and be stubbornly committed to treating others not necessarily as they are, *but as they could be.* People will rise or fall to your level of expectancy about them. When someone disappoints you, simply say to yourself, *"She wasn't in her right mind just then. She'll get back to good."*

Embrace a Forrest Gump-like view of the world and the people in it. Do not overcomplicate things. Be guileless and refuse to dwell on the negative. Stay positive as you focus on the good. When the cynics say, *"Well, that's just stupid,"* smile and reply, *"Stupid is as stupid does."*

Declare right now that you love the promise of your given context.

Your life will catch up to your level of rhetoric about it. Talk about how much you love school, how generous your classmates are and how exciting the opportunities of your new job are. You might be thinking, *"But I haven't started school yet,"* or, *"The people here seem cold"* or, *"But I'm not sure yet if I like this job or not."* None of that matters. Hear me now and believe me later: Your life will meet you at your level of expectation for it. What that means is, even if you have to fake it for now, you should begin to enthusiastically declare your passion and admiration for everything about the education and the opportunities that you are receiving. Your immense gratitude for the good in your life will bring you even greater good.

CHAPTER 15

What to Do When You Start to Feel Intimidated or Inadequate

No matter how self-assured you may be, every new venture can bring moments of doubt. Whether in a new school, a difficult class, a new job or an unfamiliar social situation, even people who usually feel competent can begin to doubt themselves. Know that those feelings are natural and that *everyone experiences the same qualms*. Set forth below are suggestions for when the voices of self-doubt come up.

Remember that feelings are not facts.

You have two minds: rational mind and emotion mind. Your rational mind puts you in your right mind, or within your reason-based faculties. It affords clarity and the opportunity for discernment. By contrast, your emotion mind can be fear-based. It is sometimes irrational, rash and misguided in its assessments. That is why emotions like anger (and even love) can make us stupid. We tend to think and act irrationally when emotions run high. Think about the euphemisms that you have heard before, *"He is a fool for love," "Love is blind"* or *"She went into a blind rage."*

In school, at work and in relationships you will know that you have gone from rational thinking to emotion-based thinking when you begin to speak in absolute terms such as, *"I will never get all this work done,"* or *"None of my classmates like me"* or *"I don't understand any of this"* or *"I always screw up."* Those sweeping assertions are not the truth about you and the circumstance at hand. None of them are factual. When you find yourself using any "all or nothing" characterizations, declare a time-out and say to yourself, *"Feelings are not facts. I know in my right mind that none of that is true. I will take a break now and then return to my right mind."*

Take a nap and, better yet, get a good night's sleep.

The night before I was to begin law school, I remember phoning home in a panic. I still had more than fifty pages to read, and many of those pages seemed inscrutable. Tired and overwhelmed, I cried to my dad, *"I'm terrified. I don't understand a single word of any of this. I don't think that the law is for me. I can't do this."* My father replied, *"Throw your fears out the window. For this moment, stop thinking with your weary mind and go to what you know in your heart. You are precisely where you are meant to be."* Then my dad added three words that I have invoked on many occasions since: ***"GO TO SLEEP!"***

I have come to learn that most fears are born of fatigue, and a good night's rest is often the best remedy. When thoughts of dread start to creep in or when the voice of your inner critic (*"You can't do this," "It's too hard," "What's the point?"*) starts to take up space in your head, ask yourself if you are exhausted. Chances are you need to rest. Take a break and take a nap. Be sure to get a good night's sleep, even if that means that not everything gets done tonight. Get to bed and set the alarm clock so that you get up earlier than usual to get the rest of your work done. You will be amazed at how much easier everything is when you have rested.

The smartest is the one who works the hardest.

My youngest sister Rosalie struggled in school. Her aptitudes were not the ones that are prized on standardized tests or traditional means of evaluation. Still, her work ethic was relentless. When it took her classmates an hour to finish a given homework assignment, Rosalie took four hours. When her friends would boast that a test was easy, Rosalie felt a familiar dread because for her, the test was hard.

As a child, teen and young adult, Rosalie would spend hours at the kitchen table, studying her heart out. When she became discouraged she would say to my mom, *"I'm stupid. I'm just not smart enough."* My mom would have none of that. She understood that intelligence is multi-dimensional, and that inside of her daughter was a form of genius not yet tapped. She would reassure my sister by reminding her that any "objective" criteria for gauging intelligence were impossibly flawed and that "being smart" in any absolute sense was beside the point.

Genius is overrated. Irrespective of any test score, victory belongs to the person with the tenacity and strength of heart to sit at the kitchen table and do what must be done. *"The smartest,"* my mom would say, *"is the one who works the hardest."*

Today, Rosalie is one of the nation's leading educators. She has authored books on remedial education, is an acclaimed teacher and a champion for children with learning differences. She runs a Montessori school in New York, and recently told us about a little boy in one of her classes. He felt shame because school was harder for him than it was for his classmates. Rosalie worked with the child after school, fortifying his aptitudes and his spirit. On one such occasion, my sister had forgotten her eyeglasses. She mentioned that to her student. The little boy replied with great sincerity and esteem, *"Ms. Franzese, you don't need your glasses because you see with your heart."*

Surround yourself with words and images that inspire you.

Surround yourself with messages of hope to remind you of the mightiness of your mission and the multi-dimensional magnitude of your abilities. There is a star that you are under, and you are precisely where you are meant to be. Keep words of inspiration in places where you can see them regularly.

Return to the five guideposts set forth earlier in this book. We suffer when we forget who we are and where we come from. The people who came before you struggled and sacrificed so that you could be where you are at this very moment. You belong here. Your place at the table was earned. Take your seat and settle down to do the work, knowing that the smartest is the one who works the hardest. Decide right now that you will use your life and your growing expertise to bear living witness to the legacy of virtue that preceded you.

Remember the two questions to ask at the end of each day.

First, no matter the result, did you try your hardest? If you did, that is good enough. If you did not, tomorrow is another opportunity to do your best. Maintain a wholesome discipline, taking the highs and lows in stride. The journey is long, and every step counts. When the material seems daunting, take baby steps, *but keep moving.*

Second, did you bring love into the world? If you performed even one act of kindness and brought a smile to even one person's face, it was a good day. Rest assured that the best is yet to be.

hastily prepared table I could not have been happier or more proud.

Mrs. Romanick was pregnant that year, and by March, at nine months, it was time for her to leave. My mom, knowing of my adoration, asked if I would like to give her a baby gift. I jumped at the opportunity and off to the gift shop we went. There I picked out a silver baby spoon. The shopkeeper asked if we would like the spoon engraved. My mom suggested that we put a little R on it, for Romanick. I said, *"No, let's put a little P on it, for Paula.''* *"But"*, my mother responded, *"It's unlikely that the baby will be named Paula."* Somehow, that fact was irrelevant to me. Thus, the spoon came to bear my initial.

When I presented the P spoon to my beloved teacher she looked at the engraving and with characteristic generosity said, *"How wonderful! Every time we use this I will think of you!"* I began crying tears of joy mixed with tears of sadness, because already I was beginning to miss my teacher.

Since it was her last day, Mrs. Romanick asked if I would like to help carry her lesson plans to her car. I was overjoyed to do so, but when it came time to hug my teacher goodbye, it all became too much. I began sobbing, fell to the ground and held on to her ankles for dear life. As she tried to pry me loose, I threw up on her beautiful shoes. (I had a sensitive stomach and the meatball sandwich my mom had made for lunch followed by the Hawaiian Punch chaser did not help.) Mrs. Romanick never returned to teaching.

I share that story with my classes with the fantasy that one year someone will stand and say, *"I am Roger Romanick, child of Mrs. Sylvia Romanick. I was the one who ate from the P spoon."* That day has never come, but something else magical did happen. As a law professor, when I was nine months pregnant with my first child Michael and it was time for me to say goodbye to my beloved class, my students presented me with a silver spoon set engraved in tiny letters with each of their initials. (Thankfully, they did not throw up on me.) I treasure those spoons to this day.

I sought out the Mrs. Romanick in each of my teachers for all of my remaining years as a student, and I seek to emulate her virtue and generosity now as a teacher myself. I have had exquisite teachers, and in their humanity I have found Mrs. Romanick again and again. Her commitment to excellence and decency found its greatest mirror in my treasured college professor and mentor, Peter Juviler.

Professor Peter Henry Juviler: Wisdom and compassion are indivisible.

It has been said that when the student is ready, the teacher appears. And so it was that I, an impressionable freshman at Barnard College, sat in Prof. Peter Juviler's political science seminar. Engaging, brilliant and most of all kind, he taught about the capacity of a few committed people to change the world. With characteristic humility, he never realized that he was the exemplar for all that he taught.

The greatest teachers, I think, are forces of nature; not in the form of a tornado but instead in the form of a persistent whisper on the fields of their students' potentiality. Prof. Juviler was whispering to each of us, *"Stretch, expand, embrace the possibilities. Define your first principles. Dare to believe that the good in some is the good in all. And go out and change the world, with each act of compassion, rendered one day at a time."*

Prof. Juviler had office hours on Tuesdays from 2-4pm, but with the line outside his office sometimes extending all the way down the hall, those would last often until 6, 7 or 8pm. I would sit patiently, reviewing my notes, and I couldn't help but overhear the meticulous care and presence of mind that he brought to every single student who appeared at his doorstep. However long it took, Prof. Juviler sat, captivated and deeply interested, as if he had all the time in the world and what you had to say was ripe with the promise of true brilliance. This no matter the stack of correspondence that sat beside his typewriter, and the volumes of materials organized at his feet that were a part of his impressive scholarly agenda. When it was my turn, I would sometimes begin apologetically and say, *"Professor, you must be exhausted. We can reschedule."* He would hear none of it. *"No, no, no, I am so happy to see you."* And he was.

All these years later, as I sit for office hours, often with a line of students waiting, I find myself greeting each and every one with that same, *"I am so happy to see you."* And I am. When I get weary, I remind myself that this is the art and this is the point. Our students are the future's game-changers, paradigm-shifters and last best hope. As teachers we are fortunate beyond measure because we get to be a part of their path.

The generosity that I have observed from my best teachers is with me every time I encourage my classes to commit to compassionate service. The exemplars in my life are front-mind when I teach that wisdom and compassion are indivisible—one cannot be sustained without the other. Their integrity is there when I remember, on the battlegrounds of our adversarial system, that while kindness will sometimes be misunderstood as weakness, it can be expected only from the secure. Cruelty comes from fragility.

Your best teachers will expect great things from you, and you will rise to their level of expectation.

Good teachers understand that people rise and fall to meet our level of expectation of them. My finest teachers expected great things from me, even when their estimations of my promise exceeded my own. I rose to meet them because I could not bear to let them down. Seek out teachers like that. Look for the ones who refuse to respond to the naysayers (including your own voices of self-doubt) in kind. The best teachers implicitly embrace the wisdom that German philosopher Goethe rendered centuries ago: *If we treat people as they are, we make them worse. But if we treat people as they could be, we help them to become just that.*

Carry your most treasured teachers in your heart.

Good teachers will share with you the gift of perspective. I remember hearing of the reminiscences of a monk who would make annual pilgrimages to the mountaintop, taking in the view and perspective from higher ground, only to then have to descend to work in the fields. When asked from the trenches to explain the point of those arduous climbs, he replied, "*So I can remember to carry the mountaintop in my heart.*"

I have been a professor and attorney for thirty years. For each one of those years I have carried the lessons learned from my most treasured teachers. My time spent in the trenches has obliged me to find my own answer to the question, "*Who do you think you are?*" When I answer: *I am a crusader for social justice, I am a champion of the underdog, I am a voice for those who have yet to find their own and I am a giver of hope,* what I am really saying is, *I am my best teachers' student.*

Your best teachers can be living or historical, real or fictional.

Whose student are you? Your role models can be actual or fictional, living or historical. You can stand on the shoulders of the countless giants who have come before you. Some you know and some you know of. Think about the people or characters you admire most. Learn about them. Read about them. Then take them into your mind's eye and carry them with you. When I write scholarly articles, I think of the elegance of the great jurists whose words were majestic and moving. When I prepare for the adversarial process, I embrace the integrity and passion of the great trial lawyers of history and literature. In negotiations, I imagine the statesmanship of our greatest diplomats.

We are neurologically equipped to mirror the examples of our best teachers.

We are hard-wired to readily emulate what others do. Neuroscientists describe the work of our mirror neurons, which allow us to empathize, feel and make real the experiences of others. Think of how you salivate when watching another bite into a delicious meal. Recollect the excitement you felt when watching a contestant win the million-dollar prize, or the tension in your legs as you watched a tightrope artist walk on the wire. Those are your mirror neurons at work, the same tool chest that can enable you to simulate the best practices of others.

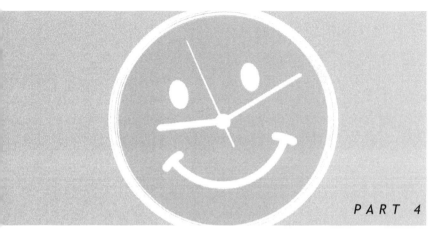

PART 4

How to Assure Your Success and Significance in School, at Work and in Life

In this section you will find a series of *"how-to"* best practices to habituate and make your own. They will assure your success and most essentially your significance throughout your time in school and beyond. Turn to each of these chapters depending on the day and the circumstance at hand.

CHAPTER 17

How to Begin Each Day

Start each day with two words: *Thank you.*

As soon as you wake up, say thank you because you did wake up. You are still here. This day is a new beginning, a fresh start, another opportunity to say what needs to be said and to do what needs to be done. This is your day to make life easier for someone else. Say thank you for that privilege.

Say thank you because you have something to do and somewhere to be. Say thank you because there is a roof over your head. Spend some time in a homeless intake center to know the despair that comes when one is without a place in this world. Say thank you because you have a good mind and a good heart. Say thank you because you have family and friends who love you.

Say thank you because you will have something to eat today. Say thank you because you will have a means of transportation. Say thank you, thank you, thank you because you have a purpose that is mighty. Say thank you to the countless people and constituencies, most still nameless and unknown to you, who are waiting for you to finish school so that you can make their lives better.

Say thank you for all the good to come. Dwell on the promise of this day. You will find that a grateful heart does not have much room for the lesser virtues.

Be guided by your heroes.

On your bathroom mirror and on your refrigerator door keep pictures of the people whose examples inspire you most. On post-its throughout your home or apartment, keep words that remind you of the promise of this world and your place in it. Our minds are constantly processing messages consciously and subconsciously. Feed your mind with words and examples of hope and aspiration.

On my bulletin board I keep the words of Dr. Martin Luther King, Jr., *"Injustice anywhere is a threat to justice everywhere."* On my laptop, I have an excerpt of President Franklin Delano Roosevelt's second inaugural address: *"Governments make mistakes. So do presidents. But the immortal Dante tells us that heaven weighs the sins of the cold-blooded and the warm-hearted on two very different scales. Let it be said that our mistakes are made in the name of compassion. Let it never be said that we have become frozen in the ice of our own indifference."*

To help my children to stay on purpose, I keep index cards with powerful messages in their sights. On my son's bedroom wall there is Booker T. Washington's wisdom, *"Let no one pull you so low as to make you hate them."* My daughter keeps *"Kindness Matters"* on her keychain.

As you step out the door, indicate your willingness to be delighted by this day.

As you leave the house, ask to be found precisely where you need to be. State your willingness to be the face of compassion for another. Indicate your readiness to be inspired by this day. Declare that you are going to seek and find the good in others. Ask to be used for a purpose mightier than yourself. If you are short for time, simply send up the quick prayer, *"Find me where you need me to be."*

CHAPTER 18

How to Take the Advice of Others

Stay true to the study methods that have served you well in the past.

You will find that many people will have lots of advice on how to do well in school or in a particular class, how to succeed at work and how to manage your interpersonal relationships. You are likely to be laden with a host of tips, pointers, suggestions and shortcuts. **Take the advice of others with a grain of salt.** In school, if there are study methods that have served you well in the past, stick with those. At work, if there is a way that you get up to speed and organize your work environment, employ those methods. If you are still learning what works best for you, be patient and know that with practice and experience you will develop an approach that is right for you.

In school, ask your teachers and professors for guidance on how to approach and summarize the material.

For guidance on how best to approach your studies, talk to your teachers. Your teachers are best-situated to share with you their expectations, what they value most on an exam, and how best to assimilate the subject matter that they teach. Ask your professors for their recommendations on former students who might be good resources. Then turn to those students who were in the class that you are now taking, who had the same teacher that you now have and who did well in the course. They will be a terrific help.

The voice in your head telling you that you cannot do this is a liar.

At times, school can be very good at fostering self-doubt. Even the most competent people will sometimes feel inadequate or unintelligent. Especially at those times, try hard to remember who you are and all that you have already achieved. That voice in your head trying to convince you that you are *"less than"* is a liar.

Being lost at times is part of the process.

To avoid doubting yourself, seek positive regard from those who know you and, in particular, those who love you. Parents can be very helpful in this context, as can other family members, close friends and old roommates. To keep your spirits up, it is important that you periodically reach out to the people who are best at helping you to maintain your sense of self and your capabilities.

Risk being vulnerable and ask someone who cares about you, *"Am I stupid? How come I'm not getting it?"* Surround yourself with people who will reply, loudly:

"YOU ARE SMART, TALENTED AND HARD-WORKING AND YOU ARE MAKING SOMETHING OUT OF YOUR LIFE. WE ARE PROUD OF YOU AND WE WISH WE COULD BE YOU! KEEP AT IT BECAUSE YES YOU CAN DO THIS AND YES YOU WILL DO THIS!"

Proclaim those words about yourself every day. They tell the truth about you.

CHAPTER 19

How to Settle Down to Hard Work

"Forget about the likes and dislikes and do what must be done."

To settle down to hard work, *settle down and work hard.* This is not rocket science. It does not matter which subjects you like and which you do not like. It is not about whether or not you are happy in this moment as you are stuck in the library while your friends are out having fun or you are working overtime on a project while everyone else is at the movies. George Bernard Shaw said it best, *"Forget about the likes and the dislikes and do what must be done. For now, this is not about happiness. This is about greatness."*

The rewards will come.

Put away your desire for immediate gratification, control your impulses to want to go to the refrigerator every six minutes or check game scores or tap into social media *and do what must be done.* The short-term sacrifice will yield long-term gains. I promise you that. In high school, college and law school, I spent countless evenings and weekends studying while my friends partied. When I started to feel resentful, I reminded myself that I was on a track to glory, that to finish this race would be to win the race, and that the rewards would come. They did. I am grateful for a career more meaningful than I could have imagined. Stay on track and stay on purpose. *The rewards will come.*

Buy your ticket.

Do not be afraid to work hard. There is no secret mystery to succeeding in school. While some of the terminology and methodology that you will be asked to apply will seem different at first, the study skills that you will need are the same capabilities that you already possess and know how to apply: reading, writing and critical thinking. The key ingredient now is hard work. That is your ticket.

There is the old joke about the man who prays every day, *"Dear God, please let me win the lottery."* Day after day, failing to win, he sends up the same prayer. Finally, angry and frustrated, he yells at God, *"Why haven't I won yet?"* By this time, God has had enough. He answers, *"Listen, I can grant your request, but first you have to buy a ticket!"*

Buy your ticket now. Resolve that you will put in the time, dedication and energy that your studies and your job require. There are no short cuts and no substitutes for that investment of time. For that matter, you would not want short cuts. The stakes are too high. You are studying and working not just for the sake of an exam or a promotion. You are learning with every challenge how to put your integrity into action.

Your work is your character made visible to others. You want the esteem in which you are held to reflect your highest and best qualities. The people who matter in your life can't see what you won't show them. Do your best. Show your best.

Set aside blocks of time and do the work.

In school, set aside blocks of time, sit at a desk with your books and laptop, and do the reading. Then think about that reading. Put it into context. Talk to your classmates about the material. Talk with your teacher about the material. Work with the teaching assistant or a tutor.

Keep your daily study and work habits uncluttered.

To habituate good study habits, keep it simple. Do not clutter your day with too many to-do lists. Mariano Rivera, the dazzling Yankees' relief pitcher and the stuff of baseball legend, described what he does this way: *"I get the ball, I throw the ball, and then I take a shower."* Similarly, keep your daily practice unencumbered by distraction.

In other words: ***Get the book and read the book. Do the work. Review the work. Then take a shower.***

CHAPTER 20

How to Create Value

Add to your stock of social capital.

Be sure to create value every day. You create value when you add to your stock of social capital by making friends, networking and giving of your time and resources to help others. Be generous for your sake. Your commitment to the good of others will bring good to you. It is what Alexis DE Tocqueville called *"self-interest rightly understood."* Do for others with the confidence that they will gladly reciprocate. **We assure our success when we help others attain theirs.**

Remember that you are no longer studying simply for an exam and no longer working solely for your own advancement.

You create value when you remain mindful of the essential truth that you are no longer studying simply for an exam. You are studying for life. Everything that you are learning will have a place in your professional labors. Even if you think you know where your career path will take you, every course matters. Each class that you take has the potential to have a significant impact somewhere along the trajectory of your long and brilliant career. Treat each course as if your future depended on it. It very well may.

Once in the workforce, remember that you are serving for purposes that transcend your own. You are working so that love can be made visible. No matter the pretext (*"I am a tech consultant," "I am a doctor," "I am a barista"*), your job is to be a giver of hope. You are doing what you do to show others the face of God, so that everyone who is fortunate enough to be in your midst might come to see that the divinity inside of you is the divinity inside of them.

Your classmates and co-workers are your colleagues. Treat them with respect.

As you look around your classes and place of work, know that the people in your midst are not only friends or classmates. They are your colleagues. They are and will continue to be a part of your professional development and future success. Never lose sight of that. You will be counting on them and them on you for many years to come. Treat everyone with respect and kindness. Build bridges. Refrain from making snap judgments or speaking ill of anyone.

The world is smaller and even more inter-connected than you might think. People's memories are long. You want to be thought of and talked about as a person of great integrity and commitment to excellence. You want people to think of you as a generous person.

Hear me now and believe me later: The impression that you make on your classmates and colleagues will follow you into perpetuity. In the years ahead, it will have the potential to help you or hurt you. Early on in practice, I needed to adjourn a deposition. Much to my relief, one of the attorneys for our adversary happened to be one of my law school classmates with whom I had always enjoyed a good rapport. I phoned him, and he graciously accommodated the request. Years later, at a conference where I was demonstrating my pedagogical techniques, an attendee stood and generously said, *"I was Paula's classmate in law school, and I am here to tell you that the kindness that she demonstrates now is the same kindness that she showed back then."* How you treat every person in your midst matters. It all comes back to you.

Create value in class and at work by being present and being prepared.

Treat your teachers, professors, colleagues and employers with respect. Show them by your demeanor that you are interested and committed to the task at hand. Be an active listener. Make eye contact and do not hesitate to nod when you are getting the point and to ask questions when you aren't.

Your teachers, colleagues and employers see much more than you think. They can tell when they have helped you to make a connection and when you are lost. They can very quickly discern when you have left the task at hand to check on a score, social media or the sale of the week. Not only will they perceive those digressions as disrespectful, but they will also lose some of their estimation of you. Your classmates and co-workers will be unfairly distracted by what you are not supposed to be doing. You cannot afford to have that happen.

Take care to be held in high esteem by the people who will be asked about you. Assume that everyone that you encounter can and will have an opportunity to share their estimation of you. I cannot begin to count the number of times that I have been asked to share my impressions of one of my past or present students. Sometimes the inquiry comes officially, via phone call or email.

More often, it arrives unexpectedly and informally, at a conference or even at a ball game or on the train. Those encounters, whether deliberate or serendipitous, speak volumes about how important it is that you make a good and meaningful impression on everyone. Be the kindest and most enthusiastic person in every room. Be the most grateful and generous student, classmate, co-worker and friend.

Be what you would want said about you.

CHAPTER 21

How to Be Prepared for Class and How to Be When You Are in Class

Bring talking points to each class.

Do the assigned readings and take careful notes. In your notebook, jot down a few talking points, or questions and comments that you would like to bring up during the class discussion. I actually began that practice in high school, and continued it through college and law school. I would always try to assert at least one of those talking points, for several reasons. First, by forcing myself into the dialogue, I was able to practice speaking publicly. You will find that every subject that you study has a lexicon and its own language. By participating in class, you help yourself to become fluent in that discourse. Second, jotting down talking points in advance of class and knowing that I would try to raise at least one of those points prompted me to read more critically and more actively. I had to pay extra attention to the materials, to the extent that my teacher or professor asked follow-up questions.

Know that your teachers see you.

Whether you are seated in a class of 100 or in a seminar of 15, your teachers see you. We see when you are engaged and attentive and when you have tuned out. We see when you have chosen to digress to do something on your laptop or phone that is not related to class discussion. We see when you are whispering to your neighbor or rolling your eyes. We see your yawns and we see your smiles.

Let your body language reflect that you are actively engaged. Sit upright. Make eye contact with the teacher. Nod when you understand the point. Listen intently and invoke what the professor or a classmate said when you make your own point. If you disagree with someone or something, state so, but always in a generous and gracious way. When you are referring to a classmate in class, use that classmate's name rather than a pronoun. For example, instead of, *"What he just said raises the problem that I too perceived,"* say, *"What James just said raises the problem that I too perceived."* Avoid all colloquialisms and be professional and respectful in your tone.

You are creating value (or not) with everything that you do (or fail to do) in class.

You want your professors and classmates to see and to think the very best of you. You do that when you adopt a respectful and kind demeanor. You do that when you are prepared. You do that when you are an active listener.

How do you want to be perceived? What are you hoping to achieve? You want to be perceived as an impeccable student and diligent soon to be professional. You want to create value and add to your stock of social and professional capital. You want your professors to think highly of you, so that when they are asked about you (and they will be asked about you, whether by prospective employers, colleagues or graduate school admissions officers), they will speak only good of you.

In class, do not use your laptop for other than class purposes.

One of the surest ways to fall in your professor and classmates' estimations is to use your laptop for other than class purposes. You will lose respect and inspire resentment. Be aware that any outside activities that you engage in are a distraction to those seated near you. That is unfair to your classmates. Remember too that your teacher sees you. Your digressions cast you as selfish, indifferent and cavalier.

Be a good classmate.

Dissuade your neighbor from digressing on his laptop. If he gets called on and needs some help, try to help. Point to where in the book he needs to be. When a classmate makes a good point, try to say so in class by weaving that point into your own contribution to discussion. After class, compliment that classmate, reiterating what a great job he or she did.

When a classmate needs the notes, be forthcoming. If a classmate is sick for more than a day or so, reach out and extend support. Offer your notes. Ask what else you might do to help.

If a classmate seems down, be particularly kind. When a classmate has reason to celebrate, share in his or her joy. When you think a good thought about a classmate, say it out loud. Remember classmates' birthdays. Celebrate them. Honor special occasions.

Stir the pot of compassion and camaraderie everywhere you go. Seek out the good in every single person in your class. Expect to find it and you will.

Be the humanity that you want to see in class.

Infuse class discussion with your idealism and generosity. Our planet's future depends on nurturing and sustaining the essential goodness that you and your classmates possess. Be firm in your commitment to think about the people behind the materials that you read.

As you participate in class remind others of the humanity and humanness of the given subject matter at hand. Put people first. Both in and out of class remember to honor your own humanness and fallibility. When you risk being vulnerable by revealing some of your own struggles and imperfections, you give others permission to do the same.

Be a leader of your class.

Organize efforts that will allow you and your classmates to celebrate the wins and commiserate when the load is heavy. Have bagel Fridays, remember each other's birthdays and milestones, surprise your teacher with the snack or beverage that he or she seems to like and place it on her desk, find local places that are fun and get the class together there on a regular basis. Organize trips to the local soup kitchen. Collect toys for the underprivileged. Cook or bake for a classmate who is sick.

CHAPTER 22

How to Give a Presentation or Make a Speech

Prepare carefully.

Think of your presentation or speech as telling a story. Your job is to be the story-teller. Almost as a journalist would report on an event or an issue, your mission is to communicate *who, what, when, where and why.*

Take notes on the critical points that you would like to communicate. Those notes can be as lengthy as you wish. Then distill those notes down to several key points. Number those key points (aiming to have between three and five points that you plan to make.) Put each of those key points on its own 4x6 index card, jotting down in shorthand on each card the essential terms and concepts that you wish to include in your elaboration of the given point. Memorize each of those cards.

How to make the presentation.

In advance, you will have with you your index cards of key points and you will have memorized what is on those cards. When the time comes to present, **have those cards with you but put them down.** Turn to them only for reference when you need to. Indicate to your audience (whether it is the professor, the class, a panel of judges, a group of colleagues, a meeting with clients or any other group) that you have three (or four or five) essential points to make. That will add an order to your presentation and it will keep the listener's attention as he or she waits for the points to advance.

Do not be wedded to a script.

Dr. Martin Luther King's historic 1963 speech on the mall in Washington, D.C. had been carefully scripted. It was only when Mahalia Jackson, a dear friend of the Reverend's, began yelling from the choir, *"Martin, tell them about the dream!"* that Dr. King ventured off script to speak to the great vision that became a cherished part of our nation's history.

Prepare your key points and have them on index cards in front of you, but do not be wedded to those cards. When you are beholden to a script you are no longer in the moment. You want to be carefully prepared but also fully present. That way, you can be spontaneous and reactive when the opportunity strikes. When you are in the present moment, you are also more likely to make a connection that deserves mention and to know when to give a particular point added attention or less emphasis.

Be responsive to the verbal and nonverbal cues of your audience.

At all times during your presentation, you need your wits about you and your emotional intelligence fully functioning. You want to be responsive to the verbal and nonverbal cues of your audience. Are the intended listeners listening, or do they seem distracted or restless? When the latter seems to be the case, be brave enough to switch course. With practice, you will soon be able to respectfully make statements like, "*I may have lost your attention. Please allow me to state the matter somewhat differently,*" or, "*It seems that it might be more effective for me to move away from this point and onto the next.*"

Honor the art in you, and not you in the art.

Leave your ego at the door. That way, you become less self-conscious because once you leave your ego out of it, the presentation is no longer about you. It is about telling a story and touching the minds and hearts of the listeners. It is about leaving the room better than when you entered, because you were there.

Whether you shine or flop does not matter. What matters is that your intent was noble and that you learned from the experience. You will be even better next time. Keep at it. Repetition is the key to mastery.

CHAPTER 23

What to Do in Classes That Leave You Uninspired

If you are feeling alienated or lost in some classes, speak up.

Sometimes, the value of good teaching is not emphasized enough in school. If you are feeling uninspired or confused, speak up. Do not let the tenor of any classroom experience silence you or cause you to be complicit in the silencing of another.

When you feel disconnected from the material or disaffected in class, have the courage to raise your hand and communicate your concern. Alternatively, arrange to speak with the teacher privately. Make your point respectfully and back it up by your careful reading of the assigned materials, but **do make your point.** Do not allow any classroom exchange to make you feel small, and never raise your hand to try to make the teacher or another student feel small.

Be clear about your intent before you raise your hand in class. Set as your intent the desire to add to the caliber of discussion in an intellectually honest and principled way. Do not raise your hand simply to show off or cause harm.

Your intention is the single most important thing that you bring to any context. Make sure that your intent is to be a virtuous contributor. Have you raised your hand to show off or to show up the teacher or a classmate? Then put your hand down. Have you raised your hand to make a principled point, add clarification, seek clarification, facilitate mutual understanding or introduce compassion and the moral referent? Then keep your hand up and speak up often. Remember that whatever you intend is what you yourself will reap. When your intent is virtuous, you will be perceived as such and you will reap virtue's rewards.

Ways to be a principled voice of reason and compassion in class.

Here are some helpful and considerate ways to add meaning to class discussion when it seems that something is missing. Each of these suggestions can help to provide a conduit for enhanced exchange. Allow them to help you to arrive at a working lexicon within which to communicate your perceived shortcomings with the dynamic at hand or your own difficulties in contributing meaningfully.

- *"The assigned readings tell the story of a group of people whose lives are forever changed for the worse because of _____. How do we reconcile that with the aims of justice?"*

- *"I understand the rule, but how does it apply in real life? When and how would we use it?"*

- *"In listening to this exchange, I'm noticing that many of us (including me) find it hard to talk about these issues. Maybe that's because we haven't yet found a way to articulate our thoughts without potentially causing offense or risking being misunderstood. Can you help us to develop a helpful vocabulary and skill set to talk about these emotionally-fraught issues?"* (This sort of concern is very relevant in classes that get to issues of bias, discrimination and other charged socio-political issues.)

- *"It feels as though this author's thesis has divorced a sense of humanity from the resolution of the matter at hand. Here's my basis for that perception. Am I right, and, if so, how would we remediate that?"*

- *"Social scientists are not automatons. They are people. It seems that the statisticians' own biases may have influenced the outcome here. Here's my intuition about that. Could I be right?"*

- *"There are many ethical and moral issues implicated by this topic. Just because someone has a right to do something doesn't mean that it is the right thing to do. What would have been the right thing to do in this case? It seems to me that a better outcome could have been achieved, but I'm not sure how."*

CHAPTER 24

How to Be a Generous Classmate, Co-Worker and Friend

The key to being a good classmate, colleague and friend is reducible to two words: **Be generous.** Commit to the practices set forth below, for others' sake and for your sake too. In a world of infinite possibilities, you do not get what you want. *You get what you are.* A generous person lives in a generous world. A person who rejoices in another's achievements assures his own success.

What you think about most is what you will move towards. Look for the excellence in your midst and seek to emulate it. Think about what you admire in others, and emulate that. Your life will follow the patterns of your predominant thoughts. You can choose those thoughts. Choose to celebrate achievement, your own and others.' Choose to exalt in the many causes for hopefulness. Proclaim those loudly. The faultfinders seem so prevalent only because they are so noisy. Move away from that cacophony of grievance and lead the team of cheerleaders for the good.

Be generous with your knowledge.

If a classmate gets called on and is struggling, subtly try to help, perhaps by pointing to the right spot in the book or whispering the answer. When I see this happening in my classes, I smile, because it tells me that my students are forming a community and building camaraderie. I want that collective spirit to be anchored in the truth that success is contagious. We get it from each other.

If a classmate asks for your notes, share them. If a classmate asks for help with some of the material and you are able to give that help, give it. If a co-worker has questions, patiently answer them. Do not fall into the trap of believing that success is limited, and that yours can only be assured at the expense of others. That is nonsense. Moreover, the ultimate measure of your success and significance in school and beyond will be the content of your character. You will be treasured and held in the highest esteem because you were kind and generous. You endeavored to help when you could. You were a team player.

Be generous with your praise.

When a classmate, colleague or friend does well, be happy, truly happy, for him or her. Communicate that joy and be generous with your praise. Jealousy always backfires. It never hurts the other, but it always hurts you. Let others' success inspire you, not deflate you. Learn from and emulate the example of successful people.

By reveling in another's achievements, and thinking about and speaking about those accomplishments with great excitement, you are signaling that that is what you admire. Your life will move in the direction of what you admire when you keep your positive regard there. *Like attracts like.*

Be generous with your sphere of influence, opportunity and goodwill.

Perhaps you have a cousin who is a prosecutor, and a classmate whose life dream is to work in the prosecutor's office. Make the connection on behalf of your classmate. Maybe a friend in class is very interested in doing marketing for a sports franchise. Because you attended a networking reception, you met someone who works for Major League Baseball. Tell your friend about that person and see if you can help to make the connection for him or her. By sharing your social capital, it appreciates in value.

In your travels, be interested in the people around you. Everyone has a story to tell and something to teach you.

You never know what the person sitting next to you on the train might mean to you or someone in your midst. I always strike up conversations on trains, planes, at airports and on long lines, with the hope that the person I meet might be able to help my students in some way. Time and again, that hope is realized. On a flight to Los Angeles I sat next to a filmmaker who I put in touch with one of my students interested in practicing entertainment law. On a train to Boston I met a practitioner based in Philadelphia who became a mentor to my student seeking to do employment law there. The list goes on. Here is the other unintended consequence of my making a habit of reaching out on others' behalf: my own life has been enriched in countless unexpected ways. By helping others grow in stature, my own success has been assured. There is a force that meets good with good.

You will grow in stature the more you help others grow in theirs.

Prof. Adam Grant, an organizational psychologist who teaches at the Wharton Business School, has engaged in considerable research and best practices that make plain that "giving is the secret to getting ahead." The New York Times Magazine recently reported on Prof. Grant's work this way:

> "Scores of studies and personal case histories suggest the benefits of an attitude of extreme giving at work. Many of the examples—the selfless C.E.O.'s, the consultants who mentor ceaselessly—are inspiring and humbling, even if they are a bit intimidating in their natural expansiveness. These generous professionals look at the world the way Grant does: an in-box filled with requests is not a task to be dispensed with perfunctorily (or worse, avoided); it's an opportunity to help people, and therefore it's an opportunity to feel good about yourself and your work. 'I never get much done when I frame the 300 e-mails as 'answering e-mails,' Grant told me. 'I have to look at it as, How is this task going to benefit the recipient?' Where other people see hassle, he sees bargains, a little work for a lot of gain, including his own". ("Is Giving the Secret to Getting Ahead," The NY Times Magazine, March 27, 2013).

By practicing altruism for its own sake, Prof. Grant has enhanced exponentially his own success. His generosity is reciprocated in countless, often unforeseeable ways. His research makes plain that what we do for others we do for ourselves.

Self-interest rightly understood.

Be generous for your own sake. Systems of reciprocity (or "one hand washes the other") are always at work, and what you do for others will be returned to you in kind. The value that you create in school, at work and in relationships will yield dividends for many years to come. Because you are held in high esteem, when a former classmate needs to make a referral on a matter outside his expertise but within yours, he will refer you. When a colleague learns of an opportunity in the city of your dreams, she will help you to make the connection.

No matter how vast the world seems, everyone is within six degrees of separation from everyone else.

We are all connected. Assume that everyone you know also knows everyone else. You want good things said of you. As you ascend, whether running for office, up for a promotion, receiving a prestigious appointment, being named leader of a company, releasing a book, receiving a prize, making a discovery or opening a new art gallery, the press and the fact-checkers will swoop in to learn more about you. They will interview your former teachers, classmates, co-workers and friends to gain a better measure of you. You will not be able to control who they choose to talk with. You want to create a record of achievement and character that you do not have to worry about. You want good things said about the person you were, because that will inform the public's perception of the person you are.

CHAPTER 25

How to Make
Penne Vodka

Preparing penne vodka can help you to be generous. Get your family, friends and classmates together to cook. This chapter, while outside the province of most schools' curriculum, will come in handy to the extent that you wish to prepare a wonderful meal.

Later in his life, my dad became an acclaimed chef. In the 1970s at Orsini's Restaurant in New York City, he was asked to prepare a pasta dish tableside for two of the eating establishment's more esteemed patrons. My dad obliged the request, and began to create a sauce with a tomato and cream base. He needed to reduce the sauce just a bit. On a whim, he tossed his glass of vodka (inspiration that he kept nearby) into the mix. The sauce let off the most enticing aroma, immediately inspiring patrons to ask, "Luigi, what are you preparing?" My dad replied in a flash, "Penne a la Russia, because of the addition of fine Russian vodka." Penne al la Russia caught on quickly, and within a few years became a staple on Italian restaurant menus in New York City. In turn, my dad enjoyed his fifteen minutes of fame on the talk show circuit, where he prepared the dish to the delight of late-night viewers.

In its later iterations, the dish came to be known as penne vodka. This is the original recipe, as devised by my dad and told by my mom:

Ingredients:

- 1 tbs olive oil

- 1 medium onion chopped

- 2 large cans of crushed tomatoes or tomato puree and 1 can of water

- 1 pint of heavy cream

- ½ cup vodka

- ¼ tsp red crushed pepper

- ½ pound freshly grated parmesan cheese

Method:

- Melt butter and oil in heavy pan over medium heat. Add chopped onion and sauté until translucent (approximately 8 minutes). Stir throughout.

- Add tomatoes together with 1 can of water and cook on low heat for 25 minutes.

- Add heavy cream, vodka and red pepper. Add one handful of parmesan cheese to sauce and stir well.

- Boil until thickened (2 minutes).

- Only add salt after you taste the sauce, and then add salt to taste.

- Cook pasta al dente in large pot of water, adding salt and 1 tsp. olive oil to the water to prevent the pasta from sticking.

- Drain well. Pour sauce over pasta and toss well.
- Sprinkle with cheese.

CHAPTER 26

How to Be When You Are Outside of Class and Out of the Office

In the hallways, elevator and cafeteria.

Make it a habit to make eye contact with everyone that you encounter. Smile at every person you see. Greet the security guard at the door with enthusiasm because you are happy to be here today. If you do not feel particularly happy, act like the most joyful person in the world anyway and watch what happens. You will be met at that level of expression, and soon have reasons to be glad.

Strike up conversations with everyone. Say hello to the people you know and those you do not yet know. Greet everyone on the administration and staff. Acknowledge the hard work of the janitor who is cleaning the halls. Thank the postal carrier who comes in with the mail. Express your appreciation to the person who made your sandwich and thank the cashier who rings you up.

When you are thinking something complimentary about someone, say it out loud. For example, if you notice that a person in the elevator is dressed exceptionally well, say so. If you bump into a professor who just released a new book, congratulate him or her. If you run into a colleague who was just quoted in the Wall Street Journal, mention it and extend congratulations. (Unless the article indicates that he was just indicted.)

It does not matter whether you formally know the given person to whom you are directing a compliment or not. When you are thinking something kind about another, snap out of your self-consciousness and tell them. Like any other habituated practice, you can make noticing the good, and saying it out loud, a habit.

In every context, see what needs to be seen. Notice when someone needs a hand, and then offer to help. Notice when a classmate or colleague seems down, and offer an encouraging word. Notice when the person emptying the waste baskets seems exhausted, and buy her a cup of coffee.

In restrooms.

Do not say anything in a public restroom that you would not want repeated. Public restrooms are public, and while you are at the sink washing your hands and commiserating with a classmate, co-worker or friend, chances are that someone is behind a stall. You do not know who that person is, and you do not want to compromise yourself or anyone else by saying something that is simply not worthy of you.

I was using a restroom in a restaurant in New York when two women came in and began speaking disparagingly about a colleague of theirs. I knew that colleague. At the sink I said, "*I know the person that you are referring to. I will not tell him anything of what I just heard, but the next person who overhears you could.*"

In public settings.

In every public or quasi-public space on or off-campus and at work, expect that everything that you say can and will be overheard. That rule applies when you are in school and in the library, student center and cafeteria. It applies when you are at an airport, train station, grocery store or shopping mall. Certainly, do not say anything that you would not want repeated. Be particularly mindful of this rule when you are on the phone.

Phone users submit to the delusion that only the person on the other end of the line can hear them. Remember that when you are on the phone, everyone around you can hear you. Exercise good judgment. Be quick and to the point until you can speak with the other privately. This will become even more important as you grow in stature and the stakes get higher. Whether on a train, plane or stuck in an airport, do not say anything to another that you would not want overheard by a reporter, a judge, a colleague, a competitor or anyone else. It is a small world, and you do not know who the person in the next seat or the next row could be.

At social occasions.

In social settings, do not drink to excess. Do not become sloppy and end up saying things that you do not quite remember but still hope to forget. Certainly, NEVER DRINK AND DRIVE. A driving under the influence charge will compromise your record in significant ways.

On your way home from school or work.

On the way to catch your train, do not rush past the homeless man or woman who needs a dollar. Give. At the traffic light, do not avoid making eye contact with the man begging for change. Give. There is likely to be a sea of need right outside your doorstep. Do not become desensitized to the suffering of others. Do what you can to help, whether in the form of a sandwich, a cup of coffee or some change or dollars that you have to spare.

"But," you might protest, *"He's only going to use the money to buy alcohol or drugs."* Maybe, but whatever he does with your donation is his business. *Your* business is choosing to give. You stir the pot of compassion every time you choose generosity over complacency. Your kindness will inspire others. You will be caught in the act of generosity and people will be moved to follow your example. Every kind deed matters.

How to Talk About Your Day

Speak good things about your day.

When you are asked, *"How was your day?"* think before you issue a perfunctory response or launch into a litany of complaints. What you think about most and talk about most is what you move towards. To talk about what went wrong keeps you moving in that direction. You have the power to change course by choosing to think about, and talk about, what went right during the day. For example, *"I had a really great science class today,"* or, *"I met such an interesting person on line in the cafeteria,"* or, *"I am the luckiest person on earth and so thankful to be in school, working toward an amazing future."*

You can curse your day by thinking and speaking ill of it or you can choose to view your day's efforts as a privilege and an immense opportunity to act in furtherance of the only two things that really matter: learning and loving. If at the end of each day you accomplished some of both, it was a good day, no matter what.

Be hopeful when you speak about your day.

It takes more courage to be an optimist than it does to be a pessimist. To seek out cause for hopefulness is to risk disappointment. Be brave enough to be hopeful. Persist in that hopefulness no matter the temporary setbacks.

If the day was just not your day, remember that it is *the day that was.*

The great news is that tomorrow you get another chance to be better, stronger, wiser and kinder. Refuse to dwell on whatever went wrong earlier in the day, and set about the task of self-correction if appropriate. Maybe you were called on in class and you simply were not as well-prepared as you could have been. Resolve that the next time that you are in that class, you will get back in the game by being particularly well-prepared and raising your hand often so that your teacher sees your effort.

Maybe you said some unkind things to someone. Send that person an apology. Decide how you will make the situation better.

Maybe this simply was not your day. Like the baby's bib says, "*Spit happens.*" If matters are within your control, fix them. Otherwise, look for the silver lining. It is there, even though that may not yet be readily apparent. Trust that you are protected, that the angels are cheering you on and that you are precisely where you are meant to be. Shift your focus away from all that is wrong to everything that is right. A grateful heart will not have room for self-rebuke or second-guessing.

CHAPTER 28

How to Talk About School, Your Job and Your Life

Declare that you love school, your work and your life.

Your experiences in school, at work, in love and in life will match your level of rhetoric about your experiences in school, at work, in love and in life. The world rises (or falls) to meet your level of expectation. Every day, state emphatically that you love school, your job and the people in your life. Sure enough and soon enough, reasons to be right about your declarations will start showing up.

Your experiences with anything or anyone will follow your thoughts and words. That is an important but subtle point to take to heart. Eventually, you will always find what you are looking for. Take good care, then, in directing your search. If you search for reasons to be hopeful, you will find them. If you look for reasons to be unhappy, you will find those.

In my own life, I have devoted three decades to seeking out the virtue and great promise of the law. Consistently, I have found it. Even in the face of setbacks, I have persisted in believing and proclaiming that the law is a noble profession. My experiences have met me at that level of expectation. I have found honor and valor even in the most unexpected places.

An enthusiastic person will always have experiences to be enthusiastic about.

A loving person will live in a loving world. By contrast, an angry person will always have something to be angry about. The cynic will be vindicated in his cynicism. Choose to be the eternal optimist. To the extent that you are called a Pollyanna because of your hopefulness, say thank you. Pollyanna was not the naïve, doe-eyed "yes" person that some try to portray. She was actually an exceedingly intelligent mediator and peacemaker. Her virtue and tenacity moved mountains. So will yours.

Do not confuse cynicism with discernment.

Do not make the mistake of confusing cynicism with discernment. Some will suggest that the world and the people in it are more often rotten than good. Do not believe that. It is simply not true.

The cynic's indictment is more than misguided. It is a form of cowardice. Be brave enough to believe that life is beautiful and that people are good. Know that even in the face of disappointment, you are strong enough not just to love, *but to persist in loving*.

Be what you want to see.

Focus most on what you want more of. Do not dwell on what you want less of. No matter where your work finds you, do your job with passion. Declare your esteem for your co-workers and your gratitude for the opportunities that this job is bringing into your life. No matter how seemingly humble your position happens to be, do your work with grace, dignity and elegance.

Persistently speaking good things about your life will bring more good things to speak about your life.

Extricate yourself from conversations that are not worthy of you. Fight the impulse to want to criticize the people in your midst or to speak badly about yourself or your circumstance. When something goes wrong, decline the temptation to want to talk about it again and again.

The choice to stay positive will require a steady resolve on your part. Our brains have been conditioned to go to worry and pessimism as the default settings. Retrain your mind by persistently thinking about and talking about what is going right.

You are the conductor and not a passenger on your train of thoughts.

Take the wheel and steer your thoughts in the direction of your dreams. Your thoughts are the predicates to your words, and your words ordain your actions. Choose what you think and what you say wisely. Your experiences will mirror back to you your level of rhetoric about them.

Do not wait for good things to happen before you start to talk about good things happening. Start now, wherever you are and whatever you are doing, to proclaim loudly and relentlessly all that you are happy about and thankful for. Get excited about all the good to come. Be expansive and be generous in your estimations of yourself and others.

Instead of, *"I am so tired,"* try, *"I am so excited about this weekend, because I will get to catch up on some sleep."* Instead of, *"I am so fat,"* try, *"I am so excited about the new gym that just opened up near my apartment. Even if it's only for ten minutes at a time, I am getting on that treadmill because I am an athlete in training. It doesn't matter how fast I go. What matters is that I go,"* and instead of, *"I hate my job,"* try *"I am grateful to have this job, and every day as I seek out the good in others I find it."*

It takes only three weeks to make a habit or break a habit. You can habituate positive thoughts by practicing them reliably for twenty-one days. You can create healthy habits by committing to them, persistently, for three weeks. That is a blink of an eye in the scheme of things. Decide now to be the boss of you and the manager of your life.

CHAPTER 29

How to Talk About Others

Do not talk about others unless you have something nice to say.

When you do have something nice to say be sure to say it. Be brave enough to make it a habit to communicate to people the admiration, esteem and respect that you have for them. It takes courage to do that because we are afraid that when we tell people the positive things that we think and feel about them they will think that we are a fake. Let go of that fear and know that if you are honest and authentic in your praise, you will be perceived as honest and authentic.

Compliment your classmates when they do a good job in class. When a teacher inspires you, say so. When you observe an act of kindness, acknowledge it and talk about it. In school, at work and in life, if you admire qualities in another, communicate your appreciation. Do not let the naysayers dominate the discourse. Contribute positively, allowing what you say to lift people up rather than bring them down.

147

Assume that everything that you say about another person is going to be repeated to that person and attributed to you.

Do not gossip. Too many bridges can be burned that way and too much drama generated. You do not have time for that nonsense. Do not say anything about another that you would not want repeated. If you find yourself about to say something that is petty or mean-spirited, stop yourself, even if it is in mid-sentence, and turn the statement into something positive. When you have something nice to say about another person, say it often. That too will be repeated and attributed to you. That is how bridges are built. It is also a way to assure that your life will run smoothly.

Do not talk *about* a person who has hurt your feelings. Talk *to* that person.

If someone has done something to upset you, wait until you are calm to choose whether and how to respond. Do not do or say anything while you are still angry. Your anger will make you stupid. Instead, cool off, not by venting but by going for a walk, a run or to the gym.

When you are back in your right mind, ask yourself whether the person who offended you is apt to be a recurrent part of your life. If the answer is yes, then get in touch with him or her. Reach out and speak your peace calmly and quietly. Give whomever it is the benefit of the doubt. Maybe she did not know better. Maybe it is all a big misunderstanding. Maybe she wanted to hurt you. Whatever the motivation, every intention has to return to its source. No doubt you have heard before that *what goes around comes around, we reap as we sow and every dog has his day.* Those are truisms because they are true. A person who deliberately hurts others cannot help but hurt himself. What we do to others, we do to ourselves. You do not have to do anything to assure that result, in the same way that you do not have to do anything to make gravity work.

Remember that you cannot control anyone else's actions. You are the boss only of you. Take charge of your reactions. Explain your position, and then move on. Be informed by what the other person did or did not do, but do not be diminished by it. While it may have hurt you, it can only continue to hurt you if you let it. For your sake, *let it go.*

If someone has slighted you, do not complain to others about it.

Do not go to people other than the source of your displeasure to gossip or complain. *"But it's not gossiping,"* you protest. *"I am simply venting."* Ask yourself if that is really true. What is your real intention when you tell the story, whatever that story happens to be? Most likely, it is to put the offender in a bad light, to hurt him by compromising others' estimations of him while adding fuel to the fires of your indignation.

Again, remember that every intention returns to its source. When you act with the intent to hurt another, you cannot help but hurt yourself. For that matter, you have no control over what the people you have "vented" to will do with the information that you have shared. The material that you shared could be used to your great disadvantage. Your confidante might be anything but, and proceed to tell even more people about your tale of woe. As the story gets disseminated, it cannot help but get distorted at your expense. Moreover, it is no longer yours to remediate. If and when you and the offender make amends, the world at large is still involved and the matter lives on.

You do not want to compound any trespass against you by making it public knowledge. The matter is between you and the person who caused you offense. Take it up there, using the first person when you explain why you are hurt. For example, *"I learned that you said some unkind things about me and that hurt my feelings. What happened?"* or *"I felt left out when I heard that you organized a night out but didn't invite me"* or *"I am disappointed that you never responded to my texts asking for the class notes that I missed."*

It takes courage to communicate your feelings, especially hurt feelings, to another. You have to be willing to be vulnerable. Take the chance and let the person know what is in your heart. You will grow stronger in character and spirit every time you stick up for yourself. By communicating that you have feelings and those feelings were hurt, you give others permission to do the same. You give the person who hurt you a chance to explain, apologize and maybe even learn from the experience.

Never respond to incivility in kind. Be a class act. Say what needs to be said, and go on your way. You have more important work to do than to dwell on another's misdeed or participate in another's low-mindedness.

PART 5

Finding Your Career Path, Applying for Jobs and Handling Rejection or Criticism

CHAPTER 30

How to Find Your
Career Path

You do not need to know what you want to do. Uncertainty is your greatest ally. Use it to stay receptive to all opportunities.

Maybe you know your desired career path. But it is more likely that you don't. Whether you have an idea of what you would like to do or not, remain open to all of the possibilities that a good education provides. Say yes to every opportunity to use what you are learning to be of service to others. I assiduously cultivated that habit throughout all of my years in school. In middle school I helped our seventh grade teacher raise awareness on behalf of a local institution for the disabled. In high school I volunteered at a nearby veterans' hospital. In college, I led a host of campus initiatives. Each experience helped to inform my range of options and helped me to know what I loved doing and what I really did not enjoy doing.

In law school, I applied for every internship, externship, *pro bono* project, clinic, research assistantship, moot court, journal, student leadership post and teaching fellowship available. I served

153

in the public sector and in the private sector. Each experience led me to the next, and provided the basis for a process of elimination. I loved doing housing reform work, but was not well-suited to criminal prosecution or defense. I loved to teach, but did not have an aptitude for corporate transactional work. I was inspired by first amendment values and media defense work, but less so by securities fraud law.

It is does not matter that you are unsure about what you would like to do with your degree. In fact, that uncertainty is your biggest ally. Use it to stay receptive to all opportunities. Say yes to every chance to serve. For every endeavor, try to be the most prepared person in the room.

Commit to the task that is right in front of you wholeheartedly. Be guided by the people you admire. Ask to be used for a purpose mightier than yourself. Do all that, and your calling will find you.

Diversify your portfolio.

Take lots of different classes and try lots of different contexts in which to serve. I began law school with the vague inkling that I would be doing public interest criminal defense work. I spent a semester doing just that for a criminal justice clinic and quickly realized that the context was not well-suited to my strengths. I worked on behalf of Volunteer Lawyers for the Arts and I loved that work, because it involved lots of negotiating and contract drafting. When I served low-income tenants and displaced families on behalf of Morningside Heights Legal Services, I knew that housing reform would become a part of my life's work.

Think of your years in school as presenting you with a vast buffet of classes and experiences to choose from. Do not be a picky eater. Fill your plate with gusto and with an open mind. Try new things. By a process of elimination, you will come to know what you love, what you like and what is simply not for you.

Stay on purpose by seeking to be of service. Show up by giving 100% to everything that you do. Stay alert and be present. Your calling—the work that makes your heart sing—will speak to you, sometimes loudly but often in the form of a whisper. Be attentive enough to hear its call. Believe that you were born for a purpose even mightier than you could have imagined, and know that your path will rise up to lead you to it.

Seek out mentors.

Attend panel presentations, guest lectures, and lots of receptions and events where you are likely to be in the presence of people whom you aspire to be like. Seek them out as mentors. Be forthright and introduce yourself, or ask one of your teachers or professors to help you to make the introduction. Ask people you admire to be your mentors. Meet with them, seek to shadow them at work for a day, learn how they got to do what they do and let their example inform your own path.

Surround yourself with virtuous, career-minded friends.

Select a circle of friends whose choices raise you up rather than bring you down. Make certain that every person in your life is high-minded, honest and true. In a world where people make snap judgments, you will be judged not only on your merits but also on the basis of the esteem in which your closest associates are held. The old adage that *"birds of a feather flock together"* means that whether fair or not, others will ascribe to you the characteristics of your friends. Be sure that your choices reflect well on you.

Do not allow your friendship with anyone to compromise your integrity or cause you to make bad choices. Do not seek immediate gratification at the expense of long term gain. Do not put yourself into a position where your life takes a brutal turn simply because you were at the wrong party, in the wrong car or in the wrong place at the wrong time.

CHAPTER 31

You Deserve to Be Happy

When you find what you love, do it.

Joseph Campbell famously said, *"Follow your bliss."* Do what you love. When you find the path that makes your heart sing, take it. There is nothing selfish or hedonistic about making yourself happy. Your happiness serves the world. Every atrocity committed in the course of human history has been committed by people who were miserable. Cultivate joy, and fill your life with so much exuberance that the spillover cannot help but improve the lives of others.

Be the star of your own life, and not a supporting actor in someone else's life story.

I remember hearing one of the members of the famous Rat Pack (the group of celebrities who traveled with Frank Sinatra) observe, *"It's Frank's world. We just get to live in it."* Make your life *yours*. Do not be a hanger-on or simply a member of someone else's entourage. Follow your dreams, not someone else's.

Be big in the world.

Be big not in the way that Hollywood might define the term, but big in terms of your benevolence, generosity of spirit and magnanimity. Be the most interested person in every room. Be loud in your praise of others. Be reliably kind. Seek out every opportunity to share your success. Assiduously ask every day to be found where you need to be.

Do all that and watch what happens. You will grow in stature, influence, opportunity and goodwill. Others will see you as the aspiration statement and find hope in your example. Your success will be assured and, even more, your significance will set the world aflame.

CHAPTER 32

The Interview: How to Be When You Want to Make a Good First Impression

Cultivate a posture of optimism.

Political strategists coach candidates to think two thoughts before making a public appearance: 1.) *I am really happy to be here* and 2.) *I have a secret*. The former is based on the premise that people are drawn to and trust those who are optimistic. The latter endeavors to cultivate on the actor's part an expression of brimming expectancy. That expression generates in the viewer's mind's eye the impression that this person is interesting and has something worthwhile to share.

Try that technique just before you go in for a job interview, a networking reception, a presentation and any other setting in which you aim to make a good first impression. In the mirror, practice thinking, *"I am so happy to be here"* and *"I have a secret."* Notice how your smile becomes slightly impish and how your eyes start to twinkle. Behavioral psychologists confirm that the viewer's more primitive brain receptors (the medulla and cerebellum) will translate that body language into, *"Oh, I want to know what this person knows."*

Be the most interested person in the room.

If you are going for a job interview, know in advance as much as you can about your potential employer. Learn about the firm or company and learn about the person who will be interviewing you. Prepare in advance three questions that you would like to ask the interviewer.

When I was in private practice, I served as a recruiter for the law firm. Always, at the end of each interview, I would ask, *"Do you have any questions?"* If the interview was thorough, sometimes the answer was no. But more often than not, it mattered to me that the interviewee had taken the time and care to prepare some questions. It mattered that the person before me was interested in learning more and had done the research to have a basis for meaningful exchange.

Think in advance of three characteristics about yourself that you would like to communicate.

For example, you want to make clear that you are exceedingly hard-working, a creative thinker, a great researcher and a good writer. Other traits to emphasize include: you are a team player, you enjoy working with people, you were raised with a very strong work ethic, you are loyal and you understand the importance of discretion. You are a person of integrity and you endeavor to do all things with character and strength of purpose. You follow-up on all tasks and you bring a deep love of learning to every project.

On the day of the given interview or networking event, make sure that you have read the news and are up on current events.

Your knowledge of current events can fill in any otherwise awkward lulls in the conversation and can help you to respond meaningfully if the interviewer happens to bring up some recent newsworthy event. I read the New York Times every morning (like it or not, it is the paper of record for the world. Read it.) I remember going in for an interview on a Tuesday (that's the day that the Times includes its Science section.) Thankfully, I had read that day's Science section, and could venture a response when the interviewer began the interview by asking a question that was based on that section's story about the melting Arctic ice cap.

When discussing current events, avoid hot topics like politics and religion. Do not ascribe labels to yourself, such as *"I'm a Republican, or Democrat, or Libertarian, or liberal or conservative"* and the list goes on. Remember Kierkegaard's wisdom that *"If you label me, you negate me."* You want to avoid giving others the opportunity to tune you out or make snap judgments about you based on some label.

If you are attending a networking reception or other more informal business or social occasion where it will be more difficult to prepare, simply show up and be interested.

Be brave enough to introduce yourself to people, and as you meet them, be interested in learning their story. Who are they? What do they do? Let the conversation flow organically and use your emotional intelligence to determine how best to jump into that flow. Has the discussion turned to the topic of great meals? Then talk about a new restaurant that you are hoping to try. Did someone mention the HBO series *Homeland*? If you watch it, join it. If you do not, ask questions about it.

During a lull in the conversation introduce some interesting or recently trending event. Think in advance of topics that might make for light-hearted conversational fare. (Again, avoid controversial, lightning-rod issues.) For example, if you just saw a wonderful movie, talk about that (unless it happens to be one of the installments in the *Jackass* series.) You might ask whether anyone in the group happened to see that interesting story about how Chinese zookeepers are dressing up like pandas to help the animals acclimate to the wilderness. Think in advance of questions and topics that are interesting rather than tedious.

Take nothing personally.

If the interviewer or potential contact that you approach seems dismissive or curt, do not take it personally. It could be that she is preoccupied by an email that she just received, or is running behind schedule or simply not feeling well. Do not let your insecurities run amok to try to convince you that you screwed up, she did not like you, you are inadequate and a flop and so on. Say, "*I tried my best,*" and move on.

Sometimes what you think was your worst interview was actually your best.

When I was in law school, I interviewed for a judicial clerkship with a jurist I admired immensely. I prepared exceedingly well, had several points that I hoped to communicate about myself and several questions that I wanted to present to the justice. At the interview, the justice spoke for fifteen minutes about his approach to the jurisprudential challenges of the more difficult cases. It was a brilliant exposition, and all I could think of to do was nod studiously. At the end of his narrative, he stood and said, *"It was a pleasure meeting you. You will be hearing from me soon."* It was clear that the interview was over, and that there was no opportunity for me to interject with questions or talking points. I shook the justice's hand and left his chambers feeling dejected.

On the entire ride back home, I engaged in multiple variations of self-criticism. *"Why didn't you interject meaningfully?"* I did not interject because there really did not seem to be an opportunity to do that, but my emotion-based tirade could not acknowledge that reality. *"Why did you just sit there like a deer in headlights?"* Actually, I was attentive throughout. *"Why didn't you ask the questions you had prepared?"* I did not prolong the interview because the justice seemed to be in a rush to move on to something else.

When I returned home, I received a call from the justice. He said, *"It was a pleasure to meet you today. I'm sorry that we couldn't speak longer, but there was an emergent matter that I had to get to. I am calling because I would like to offer you the job."* It turned out that my instincts were right after all. During the interview, there was neither the time nor the opportunity for me to say or do more. Over time, I learned to trust those instincts, rather than resort to second-guessing or harsh self-judgments.

With patience and experience, you will learn that sometimes less is more. To get to the next opportunity, you do not always have to say everything that you had planned to say or do everything that you had planned to do. Sometimes you do not have to do or say anything to be placed precisely where you are meant to be.

I believe that each of us has a path and a destiny. Ask to be used for a purpose that is mighty and honorable. Seek to use your gifts to bring joy to the world. Be of service. Use your words and actions to ease the suffering of others. Continue to show up as a compassionate force for the good. Ask to be found precisely where you need to be and your calling will find you. Expect great things. Life will meet you at that level of expectation.

CHAPTER 33

What to Remember When You Are Rejected or Criticized

When you are rejected, it is because you are protected.

Rejection means that the given position, placement or person was not meant for you. Trust that to be true, because it is the truth. With the benefit of time's passage, you will come to know that for sure. For now, take it as a matter of faith. What is meant to be for you will be for you. You will run into trouble when you chase a path or a person that does not belong to you.

Do not pursue someone else's dream. Do not compare yourself with others. That will only yield resentment or arrogance. What comes to others is their business, not yours. Be happy for others' success. Know that success is infinite. It is limitless, and the best way to assure your own is to be happy for others' victories.

As you celebrate others' achievements and decide to be governed by what you want (rather than by what you do not want), you set in motion a set of thoughts and then actions to help you to realize those desires. Your life will always move in the direction of your dominant thoughts and actions. To be governed by your resentments or jealousies will assure a basis for even more bitterness. To be guided by the wins—yours and others'—assures more wins. That is what the truism *"nothing succeeds like success"* means. It is a truism because it is true.

Take rejection in stride.

If no one is rejecting you, you are playing it too safe. That is true in life and in love. Cast out a line, even if it feels like a long-shot, and see what comes back. You miss every chance that you do not take. Take the shot. Do your best, and if you miss, learn from the experience. Be self-corrective. Maybe you need to modify your approach. Make the necessary modifications and get back in the game.

Any form of critique or criticism is simply information.

Criticism is information. It can help you to make adjustments and modifications that render your work and performance stronger. Several years ago one of my finest research assistants was in his second year of law school and assisting me with a law review article. I marked up his research memo and then completely re-worked it to arrive at the central thesis for the piece. To his great credit, he took none of that personally and saw it instead for what it was: helpful and constructive feedback. He internalized the editing and learned from it. Later, he said, *"The give and take on this project has made me such a better writer. Thank you for that."* By checking his ego at the door, he made the process of working with him a pleasure. Moreover, he spared himself (and me) the drama that our insecurities can sometimes create. His positive attitude, relentless work ethic and fine abilities have assured his success as he has advanced from one esteemed position in the law to the next.

Do not let praise or rebuke go to your head.

Be thankful for all forms of feedback, but do not let any of it go to your head. Do not allow negative feedback to devastate you, and do not let positive feedback inflate your ego. Cultivate the discernment to know which critiques are worthy of self-reflection and which are best left with their giver.

Neutralize the critic's power to potentially throw you off your game by taking a step back and asking first, is this criticism offering relevant information about you or, instead, about the critic? Often, our judgments about others are actually judgments about ourselves. You may have heard the expression that when we point a finger, three fingers are pointing back at us. What that means is that we tend to project our own perceived deficiencies or inadequacies onto others. With time, you will develop the capability to know when to accept another's judgment and when to reject it.

The tale of the sage: know which criticisms belong to their giver.

There is the parable of the sage, an elder in her community who was well known for her capacity to respond to struggle and conflict with grace. A more cynical member of the community attempted repeatedly to diminish the wise woman's achievements and to mock her message. Throughout, the woman declined to respond or to defend herself, until one day the critic came to her front door to once again launch into his litany of criticisms. Finally, the sage answered. She said, *"Sir, if someone offers you a gift, but you decline to accept it, the gift belongs to whom?"* The hostile young man paused, and then replied, *"It belongs to the person who offered it."* *"Precisely,"* said the elder. She continued, *"Similarly, if I decline to accept your criticisms and harsh judgments, to whom do they then belong?"* The man was left speechless, never to return again.

Cultivate discernment.

Discernment is the capacity to know which criticisms to accept and which to leave with their giver. It is the wisdom to know when your self-talk is actually parroting someone else's voice that you internalized very long ago but that never belonged to you. For example, when you criticize yourself for something, who do you sound like? Gently return that voice to its speaker. Find your own voice, and use it to champion yourself and the people, causes and virtues that you stand for.

It is important that you take good care in determining which of the criticisms to come your way belong more to their giver than to you. Similarly, exercise care in your judgments of others. *You cannot admire or detest something about another person unless it reflects something that you love or dislike about yourself.*

CHAPTER 34

Know Your Worth

Remember that you are not what you are called. You are what you answer to.

Inequities persist. All -*isms,* or systems of advantage based on some fixed characteristic, plaque the educational system and the workplace just as they do society at large. Whether in the form of racism (a system of advantage based on race), sexism (a system of advantage based on gender) or classism (a system of advantage based on socioeconomic status), barriers to equal access persist. Particularly when in the presence of any attempt to invalidate your experiences, demean your worth or make you feel invisible, teach people how to treat you. Be clear about what you will and will not answer to.

The challenges that face girls and women.

There is still a glass ceiling and there continue to be forces aimed at denigrating women's power and devaluing women's experiences. Respond to those forces with a clarity of vision, compassion and cohesiveness that declares firmly, *"Call me assertive, but I won't answer to bitch. Call me a game-changer, but I won't answer to obstinate. Call me kind and generous, but I won't answer to people-pleaser. Call me busy and multidimensional, but I won't answer to 'not fully on board'. Call me an essay on grace under pressure, but I won't answer to frazzled."*

To repudiate feminism is to misunderstand it. It is the pursuit of equal opportunity, a pursuit that is all the more urgent in the midst of a rollback of previous gains to achieve parity of income and access. That access is still denied in countless venues and attempts persist, some more insidious than others, to invalidate and demean women and girls.

That devaluation is present every time the message is communicated, *"You can go this high, but no higher."* It is present in the pejoratives that are ascribed to any form of perceived weakness. *"Don't be such girls,"* the coach tells the young men on his team. It is there on the less than level playing field of interpersonal relationships that describes a man as a *"player"* and a woman as a *"skank."* Those rebukes and characterizations distort what it means to be female and poison girls' and boys' perceptions of gender-based differences.

Do not say unkind things about yourself (or anyone else).

In all areas of your life, avoid holding yourself or another to some idealized depiction of perfection. The beauty industry invests countless billions of dollars every year on advertising campaigns whose aim is to make people feel inadequate. Models are air-brushed and photo-shopped to represent a standard of beauty that is physically impossible and a conceptualization of thinness that is unhealthy. When we look at the images and realize that we are not that, we buy their products with the hope that maybe we will get closer to the aesthetic that they are peddling.

Studies show that the greater the degree of a girl or woman's internalization of the industry standard of beauty the lesser the degree of her political efficacy. Think about how many times you have held yourself back because you thought it was a bad hair day or you felt fat. Think about what you say to yourself when you look in the mirror. How many times have you said of yourself or to yourself, "*I am a hot mess,*" or "*I am so bloated,*" or "*I look so terrible.*" Catch yourself in that moment and say instead, "*If I am principled and generous today, I am beautiful.*" Snap out of your self-consciousness and decide to be present and fully seen for the virtue and talents that reside inside of you. No one else would hold you to as harsh a standard as you no doubt hold yourself. Be joyfully you, because that is what will capture people's hearts and minds.

Do not surrender your power to a bad hair day.

Listen carefully to your self-talk. How mean are you to yourself? Would you ever be that cruel to another? Think about how often you have sabotaged your day because you did not like the way you looked or maybe your pants felt tight or you got a huge pimple. Your male counterparts most likely are not trying to be invisible because of a break-out or frizz.

I remember telling my mom about a presentation that I had given, where I had talked about the promise of good government and ethics reform. As I described the talk I also told my mother, "*I don't think I looked good. My suit had gotten wrinkled on the train and my hair was awful.*" My mom asked, "*Were your remarks substantively meaningful?*" I answered that they were. She continued, "*Were you generous and kind throughout the course of the event?*" I replied that I was. "*In that case,*" she said, "**you were beautiful.**"

CHAPTER 35

You Are Already Good

No external source can be the judge of your worth. Know that you are already good.

Whenever you confront or embrace any criticism, what you are really trying to know is whether or not you are good. You await feedback from a teacher or professor to know whether you are a good student. You receive evaluations from an employer to know whether you are a good worker. You await your child's words to know whether you are a good parent.

Here is the problem with framing criticism or feedback as a way of discerning whether or not you are good: No external source, whether a teacher, employer, co-worker, friend, classmate, spouse, parent or child, can ever be the judge of your worth. To give anyone or anything the power to define you or chart your course puts you at the mercy of another's lens of perception. That lens cannot help but be distorted by the biases of the beholder.

It is up to you to know, really know, that you are already good. You were born that way, and you will stay that way. You are better, so much better, than the worst thing you have ever done. You have shined brightly and you have fallen flat. Your finest moment is yet to be. Through it all, you have been good.

Do not subject your estimation of your significance to the carelessness of the crowds.

People can be reckless and irresponsible. Do not hang yourself out in the marketplace of public opinion to arrive at your sense of self-worth. If you look to external feedback to gauge your value, you will be flapping in the changing winds of others' impressions. You are magnificent because you are. Get that through your head and your heart because if you don't, you will be chasing others' approval when you should be chasing your dreams.

You will come to see your intrinsic worth by keeping in touch with your soul. Seek out daily sanctuaries, whether found in nature, in a chapel or any other quiet place, or by reading inspiring words, meditating, listening to music, practicing yoga, going for a walk or volunteering at a local children's hospital. To remember your innate goodness, spend some time sitting with newborn babies. Be in awe of the divinity in every face, whether of a child, an elder and everyone in between. The beauty that you perceive in others is the same beauty inside of you.

Return to your own answer to the question *who do you think you are?*

In the presence of any feedback, whether good or bad, always return to your answer to the question *who do you think you are?* Keep the answer to that question close at hand, whether on an index card or on your phone. Let it resound with the truth about you.

You are a person of substance and honor. You are a voice for those who have yet to find their own. You are a giver of hope because your life bears living witness to the essential premise that what does not kill us makes us stronger.

You understand criticism for what it is: feedback that has the potential to improve your performance at something. Sometimes that feedback is helpful. Other times it is best left with its giver. Regardless, no evaluation can ever be taken as a referendum on the measure of your worth.

The inviolate truth about you is unassailable. You are worthy, you are significant and you are good. Not because of what you did or did not do, but because you are.

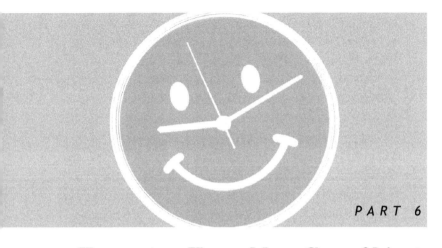

PART 6

How to Handle Conflict or Adversity

CHAPTER 36

What You Need to Remember in the Face of a Slight or Betrayal

Another's meanness is their business, not yours.

There is an inviolate, untouchable part of you that no one can ever diminish. When someone tries to hurt you, be like a puppy that gets caught in the rain. Shake it off and keep going. Refuse to hold onto the snub or insult and leave it with its giver. That is where it belongs and that is where it cannot help but end up.

The person who meant to hurt you will suffer as a consequence of his hurtful actions. You do not have to do anything to assure that result, just as you do not have to do anything to assure that the apple you drop will fall to the ground. Like the law of gravity, the law of cause and effect is always at work. Every action runs as a cause and must return to its originator as an effect.

Whatever we do to others we do to ourselves.

Whatever we do to others, we do to ourselves, in the same way that whatever we do *for* others we do for ourselves. Call it karma, the boomerang effect or the law of just desserts, but the point remains: every intention returns to its source. The expressions *"every dog has his day," "what goes around comes around"* and *"we reap as we sow"* are truisms because they are true. When you intend to hurt another, you inescapably bring hurt to yourself.

We do not get what we want. We get what we are.

In a world of infinite possibilities, remember that we do not get what we want. *We get what we are.* A hurtful person will live in a hurtful world. A loving person will live in a loving world. Give what you want to receive.

For that very reason, decline the temptation to respond to meanness or incivility in kind. The antidote to another's mean-spiritedness is never more of the same. The corrective for heartlessness is love. Love yourself enough that you refuse to carry around another's wrongdoing by holding on to a grudge or a grievance, or reliving the episode a thousand times in your mind's eye.

For your sake, and for the sake of the countless people and constituencies who are counting on you to make the difference that only you can make as a person of principle and virtue, *let it go*. Drop the chip on your shoulder. It will only weigh you down.

CHAPTER 37

Be an Instrument of Peace

Take the high road.

Sometimes, you will find yourself at odds with a teacher, classmate, colleague, employer, family member, neighbor or friend. Know this, first and foremost: your intention is the most powerful tool that you bring to any dispute or discord. Set your intention before you say another word to that person or about that person.

Do your words and actions intend to cause trouble or facilitate understanding? Is what you are about to say intended to cause hurt or to promote forgiveness? Remember that your intention will return to you. Whatever you intend, ultimately, is what you get in return. If you intend to cause pain, you will receive pain. If you intend to bring peace, you will receive peace. Thus, be clear and be high-minded about your intent.

Set as your intention the desire to promote the cause of mutual understanding, respect and goodwill. It takes only one person to defuse a conflict and to turn anger into reason and fear into calm. By contrast, to respond to meanness with more meanness is, simply put, beneath you. You are too good for that.

"*But,*" you might protest, "*I am right about this, and he is wrong. What he did was wrong, what he said was wrong, and what he failed to say was wrong.*" Maybe you are right about everything. But as the old saying goes, you can be right or you can be happy. Choose to be happy. Trust me on that. Let it go, take the high road and hold onto your perception of the agitator as he *could be* once he heeds the call of his better instincts. Do that and you help him to answer to that call. Meet him instead at his level of lesser virtue and you only make matters worse.

Do not take the bait.

"*The fish is caught because of its mouth.*" When someone dangles a worm of offense, refuse to bite. Take very good care with your words. Otherwise, you will only say or do something best left unsaid and undone. Keep swimming.

Never fight with a skunk.

I recently gave a talk where I cautioned against responding to meanness in kind. Afterward, Gerald Viturello, a public servant, shared the wisdom of his former colleague to "*never fight with a skunk.*" That says it all. If you take on the skunks, you take on the stink. Walk away.

Getting stuck in resentment robs you of your power.

Hanging on to negative judgments deprives you of the opportunity to see what is really good in your midst. Holding on to resentment puts you at the mercy of another's incivility. Do not demean yourself by responding to meanness in kind. Try to be the voice of reason and, if that fails, walk away rather than do something you will regret. Never send an email in anger, and never reduce to writing what you would not want broadcast on the nightly news.

CHAPTER 38

Let Your Kindness
Be Irresistible

Show up with a basket of muffins.

Before entering any situation that is fraught, anchor yourself in so much dignity, grace and goodness that, just by showing up, you elevate the room. Be generous and be kind. Show up with a basket of muffins or a bouquet of flowers. Your humanity will be disarming, and your presence will encourage others to show their kinder selves.

See the agitator as better than whatever he or she is doing right now.

Stubbornly see the given agitator as better than whatever he is displaying at the moment. When a colleague or adversary does something unbecoming, calmly say to him, *"I know that you are a gentleman."* Then walk away. Allow for some breathing space and let some time pass. Soon you will see that your decision to be generous in that moment was not only disarming but transformative.

Do not hold onto any indignity by thinking about it or talking about it.

Do not hold onto any agitator's trespass by continuing to replay it in your mind or by repeating it to others. Let the person who behaved poorly off the hook. How he behaved is his business and his mess. How you respond is your business. Take the high road. Free yourself from the need to convince others of how awful he is. That kind of talk will only reflect poorly on you. His words and actions will speak for themselves, and he will reap the consequences of his conduct. You do not have to do anything to assure that result. Do not dwell on what he did or did not do, and move on. You have more important matters to think about and more important work to do.

CHAPTER 39

Power versus Force

How to be persuasive.

True persuasion comes from the effective use of your power rather than force. Power comes from within. It is the quiet knowing that rightness is on your side and that it will prevail. Anchored in careful preparation and restraint, it is exercised gently and to great effect.

Force, by contrast, is rooted in weakness. It is externally-derived and can quickly devolve into coercion or, worse, brutality. It is combustible and as it explodes it becomes scattered and diffused, thereby losing precision. While it might temporarily secure certain aims, its ends are short-lived because they lack the power of legitimacy.

Use your power to calmly bring others to your point of view, no matter how long that might take. State your peace forthrightly and without hesitation. Allow for the other to rant and rave if he is so inclined. Wait for the tantrum to be done. As it spills out all over the place, do not defend and do not push back. Remember that you are using power, not force. Extricate yourself from the scene until the storm has passed and then, with the same equipoise and calm, re-state your position and your desired end.

The first person to raise his voice has lost the argument.

Our anger makes us stupid. You lose all power to persuade when you move from your rational mind into your emotion mind. Believe in the rightness of your cause and then, like a surgeon at work, be precise and deliberate in your execution. Do not allow your ego to cloud your judgment, and do not be deceived into thinking that you must fight *against* something or someone. *Remember what you are fighting for and be for that, not against something else.*

An esteemed jurist recently used the metaphor of buying a car to tell our students about the virtues of the quiet exercise of power. Suppose that you have done the research and that you have come up with the amount that you are willing to pay for a particular car make and model. Be sure that your number is reasonable and fair. Go into the dealership and present your research and your number to the dealer. Suppose that your aim is to buy the car with certain enumerated features for $30,000. Once you present your terms, the dealer might launch into a detailed recitation of all the reasons why your number is too low. Then he might engage in verbal and mathematical acrobatics to convince you why you need to raise your number. Sit tight and do not refute or defend against anything that he is saying. When he is done, calmly state, *"I will buy the car with the features enumerated for $30,000."* Then just sit there quietly. More often than not, when all is said and done you will prevail on your terms.

CHAPTER 40

How to Break Bad News

The sandwich technique.

Whenever you have to share bad news, use the sandwich technique. I learned this from one of my beloved teachers, Chara Caldarone. The first slice of bread is some bit of good or positive news that is relevant to the matter at hand. Next, state the bad news simply and without drama. That is the inside of the sandwich. Then, restate the good or positive news, making it the top slice of bread to complete the sandwich.

For example, suppose that you need to tell your parents about a lackluster grade. Start with the good news. *"Mom, Dad, I'm really enjoying school and I did so well in my history class that the professor sent me a really positive e-mail commending me for my work."* You have just set a positive backdrop against which the not so great grade is put into a larger perspective—your fine aptitude and academic promise. Then state the bad news plainly. *"I got back my science grade, and ended up with a C. I'm disappointed but I made an appointment to see the teacher and I'm looking forward to figuring out what happened and how I can do better."* Finish with more good news. *"Thank you for believing in me. I am committed to learning from this and to working even harder than before."*

The sandwich technique allows you to put your best foot forward and to conclude on that note. It works in both professional and personal realms. For example, suppose that you need to tell your client, a buyer of real estate, that the closing date on an investment piece of property has to be delayed by a week. Start with the good news. *"I am excited about closing this transaction for you. Having done the due diligence, this lot has been deemed a very solid investment."* Now break the bad news. *"I know that you are anxious to close, but I just heard from seller's counsel and we need to delay the closing by a week."* Then, conclude with the good news, *"By agreeing to the postponement, we have added leverage in the following ways."*

More personally, suppose that you have to break a dinner date. Start with the good news. *"Our friendship means so much to me. Thank you for always being there for me."* Then, *"I am so sorry but I am impossibly tied up on a deadline and I need to ask if we can please reschedule our dinner."* Close with, *"I can't wait to see you. As soon as you check your calendar, let's reschedule, sooner rather than later."*

CHAPTER 41

How to Cope With Competing Demands

You do not have to do it all and you certainly do not have to do it all at once.

If you find yourself answering to several competing demands, take a triage approach and respond to the most pressing matter first, and then continue to do what you can with the less immediate concerns. Know that you cannot be all things to all people and that you do not have to do everything that needs to be done all at the same time. For that matter, you cannot do it alone. Seek out help and support from those around you. Asking for help is not a sign of weakness. It is a show of strength. It indicates that you have the wisdom to know that no one can do it alone.

Find a good counselor or therapist to help you to cope with the difficult task of managing competing demands. It is important to have someone in your corner who can really listen to you and help to correct your perceptions when they become distorted by your own sheer exhaustion. Most schools have very helpful therapists who come to campus at least one day a week. They are licensed professionals who are obliged to keep all that you discuss confidential and privileged.

Stay away from energy suckers.

Sometimes people will try to sap your reserves of time and energy to replenish their own. Set healthy boundaries and extricate yourself from relationships that are draining. Think of the very word *draining*. **You want to surround yourself with people running on a full tank, rather than those who try to siphon off yours.**

Your competence in the world makes you a better family member, parent, child, friend and spouse.

Let your developing proficiencies make you even more generous in every role that you play. Allow your work ethic and growing confidence to inspire others. You are modeling all sorts of behaviors all of the time. See every context that you serve as a setting for you to grace by your example.

CHAPTER 42

When You or a Family Member Gets Sick

Do not become an island.

Reach out to others. Tell your school's dean of students what is happening so that the two of you can anticipate what if any accommodations might need to be made to help you to get through the semester. Reach out to your classmates and friends. Let them know what you are going through. They will rise to the challenge and carry you over the icy patches.

Do not keep your pain or sorrow to yourself. Everyone has experienced their share of heartache, and from that well of experience people will extend a hand. Accept others' help without hesitation or any form of embarrassment or shame. You will not be seen as *less than* because of your struggles. Indeed, you will be seen as *more than* whatever others thought before.

Give people a chance to be kind and generous to you, for their sake as much as for yours. Trust that a broken heart has more room, and that love brings hope.

CHAPTER 43

When You Endure the Break-Up of a Relationship

You will love again.

When the person you thought you were really crazy about decides to move on, *know that anyone who does not want you does not deserve to have you*. Who that person chooses to love or not love is his or her business. You cannot control that. You never did. We only let in the love we think we deserve. You cannot fix another.

When you have loved deeply, no matter the end, you are better because of it. Be gentle with your broken heart, and trust that you will love again. You will love again because you never stopped loving. To love is your essential nature. Do not wait for Mr. or Ms. Right to come walking through the door. Be the loving person that you are in all circumstances and in every context. That is how you get to be the star of your own life. It is charisma, and it will draw to you even more to love.

195

Do not become cynical about love.

Continue to believe in love. It will disappoint you sometimes, but be brave enough to know that you can transcend love's sorrows to once again bask in its glory. The measure of your greatness will not be found simply because you loved. The measure of your greatness will reside in your capacity *to persist* in loving, no matter the disenchantments and the setbacks.

You will get knocked down in the pursuit of love, but you will get back up. You will be called a starry-eyed idealist, and you will say *thank you*. The pessimist cannot answer to that call because he won't take the chance. Instead, he will stick to his story that life is a school of hard knocks and people stink. That way, he thinks, he cannot be hurt. *But here is the tragedy of the cynic: by closing himself off to the power and promise of hopefulness, he suffers the greatest hurt of all: its loss. Keep hope alive in your heart. Without it, you join the ranks of the living dead.*

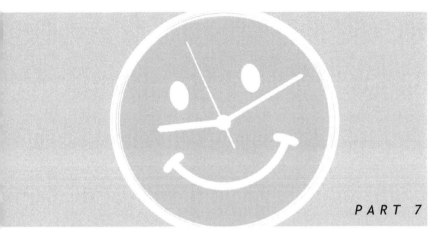

PART 7

How to Succeed on Exams and What to Do When You Feel Worried or Unsure

CHAPTER 44

Exam Preparation and Peace of Mind

Ignore the craziness in the atmosphere.

Exam time can do strange things to ordinarily kind, decent people. Competition can be fostered among some. Others retreat, feeling alienated. Some become aggressive, others cranky, and still others fatalistic. Extricate yourself from the doomsday prognosticators and ignore the hysteria and hype that midterms and finals can conjure up. You have taken many tests before, and you know what works and what does not work for you. Stay true to the study habits that have served you well in the past and abandon any practices that do not serve you.

Exams can cause even the most capable people to doubt themselves. Recognize that to the extent that you are feeling uneasy, anxious or maybe even terrified, it is not you. The system of evaluation leaves much to be desired. It has built into it features that can inspire panic. Sometimes, a whole semester's worth of work comes down to performance on a two or three hour final exam. Sometimes, the exam schedule is simply too crowded, and it will seem that there is too little time to accomplish too much.

Do what you can with the time that you have. Do not allow yourself to get psyched out by what others are doing or not doing in preparation. Play your game, not theirs.

You have the time you need.

Slow down, take a deep breath and look at the exam schedule. Prioritize and budget every hour of each day. These are conquerable matters. There are many hours in a day, and many minutes in an hour. You have the time you need.

Performance is enhanced by calm.

If and when you go into panic-mode, realize that you are most likely holding yourself to some idealized standard of perfection. Get that impossible ideal out of your head because it doesn't exist. Keep moving through the material, knowing that your work only has to be as good as it can be under the totality of circumstances in which you find yourself. Under better circumstances, your work will be better. With time, as you become a stronger writer and test-taker, your work will improve. Do your best with the time that you have, knowing that this is simply your best *at this time*. You will keep getting better and better.

Be generous to your classmates.

Anxiety and nervousness is natural. But you can rise above it. For that matter, you can let it bring out the very best in you. Hemingway defined guts as grace under pressure. Be generous to the people in your midst. Help them. Let a spirit of cooperation characterize all of your efforts, especially now. Reject any limited view of success. Success is boundless and it is contagious. There is plenty to go around.

Be kind and dignified, mindful that your classmates today will be your colleagues tomorrow. People's memories are long. Know that one year from now, indeed, twenty years from now, your classmates won't remember you as the person who got two As or two Cs first semester. What they will remember is how you conducted yourself in the process. It is who you are, and how you got there, that they will remember.

For guidance on how to conduct yourself, think about what you would want said about you at your funeral. (No, exams won't kill you. But this exercise is actually a helpful one.) When all is said and done, how would you want to be remembered? More immediately, at the conclusion of each school year, what will you have left behind? What will be your legacy? Will they be saying, *"What a competitive, win at all costs kind of guy he was. I'll never forget the time he hid that outline from his study group."* Or will you be remembered as a decent, honest, hard-working person, always willing to help when you could? Memories die hard. The associations that you are forging now will outlive the challenges of the immediate future.

CHAPTER 45

How to Be When You Feel Worried, Unsure, Inadequate or a Flop at the Task at Hand

Remember that feelings are not facts.

Say that out loud and believe it. Emotions are ephemeral. They come and go as long as you allow them to. When a feeling of dread or worry comes up, recognize that you are in emotion mind. Go back to rational mind by becoming analytical about the feeling, testing its legitimacy. For example, when emotion mind takes over and you find yourself thinking or speaking in absolutes such as *"I can't do this. There's too much here and I'll never get it done,"* gently challenge the thought by analytically testing it. Think, *"Wait a minute. You have gotten even more than this done in the past, and you have succeeded. This is conquerable. You don't have to move this mountain with one push. Let's start by removing one rock at a time."* That deductive process takes you out of emotion mind and back into your right mind.

You will know that you are in emotion mind when you are thinking and speaking in dramatic generalizations. For instance, "*I have no idea what's going on in class.*" Realize that your hyper-generalization is untrue. You do have some idea of what is going on in class. If it is a Philosophy class that finds you confused, and more specifically, it is the material on Kant that is giving you trouble, you do know the context that you need help with as well as the topics that you are comfortable with. That knowledge gives you enough of a basis to reach out to the professor and to upper class students for tutoring, supplemental reading and whatever other assistance might prove helpful.

Do not "*should*" on yourself.

When you hear yourself saying, "*I can't believe I screwed up that [exam, presentation, and so on] so horribly. Now the [teacher, my classmates, again, just fill in the blank] must think I'm a total idiot. I should have done [fill in the blank]. I shouldn't have done [you name it.]*" Right then, **STOP SHOULD-ING ON YOURSELF!** Interrupt the dramatic parade of horribles that your ego in concert with your emotions cooked up. Again, subject what you are thinking to logic-based scrutiny. The person or persons you presume judged you so harshly have already forgotten about it and moved on. Now it is your turn to do the same.

You are your own worst critic. We all are. Your perception of how something went is apt to be distorted by the lens of your self-directed strict and harsh scrutiny. If you knew it all you would not be in school and you would likely be very, very old and living on a mountaintop somewhere in a remote region of the Himalayas. Give yourself a break and congratulate yourself for getting in the game. Know that even if you get knocked down, what matters is that you get back up. You are learning and getting better every day.

Most fear-based thinking is the product either of exhaustion or isolation.

Worry is a fear-based emotion. Most of our fears are born of exhaustion or isolation. If you are really tired, take a nap and then return to the task at hand. If you feel isolated, reach out to a family member or friend. Keep nurturing books close at hand, and turn to their chapters for a quick boost. Watch a few minutes of an inspiring speech or movie excerpt. Remember that although it will sometimes feel that way, you are never alone. There is a star that you are under, and life is rooting for you.

CHAPTER 46

How to Be When You Get Stuck in Negative Thoughts

Switch the thought.

When thoughts of gloom begin to set in, notice them and then **CHOOSE ANOTHER THOUGHT.** Keep in the forefront of your mind one particular experience from the past that made you happy. Conjure up its details. Feel it. When a self-defeating thought comes to mind replace it with that happy memory. Habituate the expression *"switch"* as your cue to switch up the thought.

Athletes employ sports psychologists who teach this "switch the thought" technique. A pitcher who needs to get his head back in the game or breakaway from fear will use a buzzword or phrase (*"switch"* or *"release the mechanism"*) to re-establish his positive focus. You do the same. You are in charge of your thoughts. Your thoughts are not in charge of you.

When you are feeling deflated, it is probably because you are holding yourself to an unrealistic standard.

When it all seems like too much, realize that you are most likely holding yourself to an unrealistic standard of perfection. Abandon the quest for some brand of nuanced excellence that you have conjured up and instead simply commit to *"good enough."* As long as your performance on the exam, the paper and any other assignment is good enough, you will be fine. To finish the race is to win the race. You do not have to come in first, second or even in the top 99%. The last one to cross the finish line still crosses the finish line.

When you feel stuck in a funk, simulate the body language of a really happy person.

Change your posture. Stand taller, shoulders back and chin literally up. Start smiling and laughing. I mean it. Start laughing really, really hard. It will seem nutty, but it works. Your brain's neurotransmitters will understand your smile and laughter to mean that you are happy and in response release endorphins that will actually let how you feel match up with how you are acting.

I have a friend who teaches Laughing Yoga, a class where the members hold a posture and then laugh hysterically. I thought she (and they) were nuts, until she simulated a few minutes of the practice at our home. We all followed her instructions, stood in tree pose and then were led on a five-minute laughter explosion. The results were dramatic. Everyone's mood lifted and the various to-do lists seemed so much more achievable. By laughing at nothing, we learned to lighten up about everything. All the stuff that we get caught up in is not as important as we like to think.

CHAPTER 47

What to Do Before the Semester Ends

Read through your class notes to be sure that they are complete and clear.

Before the semester ends, run through your notes for each class. Jot down any questions or sources of confusion. Clear those up before the reading period, so that when you actually get down to the business of studying for exams you won't be in the burdensome position of having to learn material from scratch. The study period should be spent reviewing, reducing the subject matter to an accessible format, and doing practice questions.

Think offensively about what is likely to be asked.

For each subject, think offensively about what is likely to be asked. By paying attention in class, you should have a good idea of which topics have been stressed and which issues seem of particular interest to your professor. The student-teacher exchange should provide clues as to which sorts of answers the professor values. Ask each of your professors if he or she has any advice on exam-preparation and exam-taking. Listen carefully to the response.

If available, get copies of the professor's past exams.

Many schools make copies of past exams available on-line or at the reserve desk in the library. Take a look at those exams to begin to gauge the professor's likely expectations. After you have reviewed a given unit, find a former exam question that addresses that unit. Try to simulate exam conditions and do that question. Repeat that exercise as often as time permits. Ask your respective professors to comment on or critique your efforts. If the professor is unavailable, seek out the input of a teaching assistant or tutor.

Make a study timetable.

Carefully review the exam schedule and set up a master study timetable for yourself. Budget and regiment your time. Build study breaks into the schedule. Build into the schedule things to look forward to. Keep the schedule handy and consult it often. It represents an important way for you to take control of the exam period and direct your energies.

CHAPTER 48

Getting Down to the Nuts and Bolts

Take the offensive.

To maintain a healthy, positive state of mind, take the offensive. So much of the anxiety that accompanies exam-taking resides in the sense that you are no longer in control, with forces beyond you now calling the shots. Accept your power and take back control. You can take matters into your own hands by understanding more about the skills that are tested on exams.

Be mindful of the skills that are tested on exams.

An objective exam (multiple choice, typically) is testing on your mastery of the subject matter as well as your powers of discernment. You want to be able to know which answer choices to eliminate and when to select *"all of the above"* or *"none of the above."* The best way to hone those aptitudes is by practicing the format in which the exam questions will be asked. Check with your teacher to see if past exams are available on-line. See if a study aid or workbook that contains comparable practice questions is available.

Studying for an objective exam will require lots of memorization. Even if the exam is open-book, you are unlikely to have the luxury of time within which to peruse your books and notes to uncover the right answer. Have the answer in your mind's eye, and then, if the exam is open-book and time permits at the end, use the resources that you brought in to double-check your work.

Use mnemonics, acronyms, metaphors and imagery to help you to memorize the essentials. Use index cards to test your memorization of the material. Write out the key points in longhand, rather than using your keyboard. Studies show that the process of actually writing down the material helps to anchor it more effectively than typing it.

Essay exams require that you use your writing and analytical abilities to answer the questions presented. Again, study for an open book exam the same way that you would study for a closed book exam. Memorize relevant essentials and, in advance of the exam, think about how the various topics that were covered relate to each other. Ask if the professor has copies of past exams available for review.

Often, essay exams test on the student's ability to be issue-inclusive and comprehensive. For purposes of grading, your teacher is likely to have prepared a master list of all of the topics and issues that the given question was intended to raise. She will have assigned point values to each of those topics. Your exam will suffer point deductions for every issue that you neglected to mention. Thus, you want to be as issue-inclusive as possible without including extraneous or irrelevant material.

Prepare an outline for each of your courses.

The outline that you prepare for each of your classes will prepare you to spot the issues on your exam and give those issues their due. Do not fall prey to the illusion that an "outline" is some mysterious and elusive document. An outline is simply a summary of the course, organized by topic, to help you to anchor and memorize key information. Create an outline to help you to see the connections between and among the units that were covered.

To prepare your outline, have by your side your books and readings for the course and a full and complete set of class notes. It is helpful to have a copy of an upper class student's outline for the course, to serve as an example but not as a substitute for your own work. Be sure that the sample outline comes from a student who did well in the course and who had the same professor that you now have.

Using your syllabus, notes and reading list as your guide, begin building your outline. Organize it according to headings and subheadings. Include relevant excerpts from the texts and helpful passages from your class notes.

Condense your outline into a mini-checklist.

Once your outline is complete, condense it into a five to ten page mini-checklist of bullet points, again organized according to topic. Memorize the mini-checklist. When an exam is closed-book, go through that checklist in your mind's eye to be sure that you are being sufficiently issue-inclusive. On an open-book exam, you can turn to it but do not fall into the trap of thinking that you will have lots of time to peruse it. Know it so well that you do not need to spend much time looking at it, even when that option is available.

CHAPTER 49

Exam Preparation's
Seven Points of Light

1.) Be true to the study techniques that have worked for you in the past.

You know what works for you. While the format of some exams may vary, the skills being tested remain the same. Most often, you will be asked to demonstrate good writing, reasoning and analytical abilities. You will be asked to show your mastery of the subject matter and your understanding of its content. Avoid shortcuts, settle down to the task of careful preparation and do what must be done.

2.) Avoid comparisons to others.

If you keep looking over your shoulder, you will trip over what is in front of you. What others are doing or not doing is their business. Your business is to stick to your tried and true study methods and keep pushing through the material.

3.) Avoid overkill.

The temptation might be to get your hands on every possible study aid, outside resource and outline that you can find. Resist that temptation. Simplify. Unless it is a take-home exam where outside sources can be used, all you need are your course books, class notes and, if available, one good sample outline for each course.

4.) Abandon any perfectionistic tendencies that you may have.

Strive for excellence, not perfection. Even better, remind yourself that you only need to do well enough. In the semesters ahead there will be many opportunities apart from exams for you to distinguish yourself. You will take advantage of those, thereby diminishing the significance of grades.

5.) Repetition is the key to mastery.

The more you go over the material and the more times you review available past exams the more proficient you will become. That proficiency will conquer your anxiety and help you to relax.

6.) Performance is enhanced by calm.

Cognitive learning specialists confirm that retention, understanding, and performance are enhanced immeasurably by calm. There are many hours in a day, and you have the time that you need. Keep matters in perspective. To finish the race is to win the race.

7.) **Remember that regardless of the grade, the studying itself is important.**

No matter the result, you are not studying solely to do well on the final. The studying itself is important because you are honing aptitudes and developing proficiencies with every task that you accomplish. You are building intellectual muscle, and you will use that muscle to be strong in the world.

CHAPTER 50

Writing a Good Essay

Budget your time.

Often, your professors will let you know the format of the exam in advance. When that is the case, know how you will budget your time before going into the test. Once there, adhere to that time budget no matter what. When it is time to move on to the next question, move on. Your job is to finish the exam. Your grade will suffer mightily if you cannot devote the allocated time to each section of the test.

If you have not been told of the exam format in advance, once the exam is distributed take a few minutes to read the instructions to determine how many questions are presented and how many points are allocated to each. Create a time budget and stick to it.

Read each question carefully.

You are being tested on your ability to apply the course material to a particular question or questions in a thorough, issue-inclusive way. You want to read each question that is presented carefully and more than once. After you have read the question a second time, outline your response. As you are writing your answer, refer back to the question often to be sure that you are answering all that it asks.

Do not restate the question for its own sake.

As you write your answer, include the course materials that are salient to and support the points that you are making. Do not restate the question(s) asked, but be sure that your answer is focused and directed to what is asked.

When answering an essay question, be issue-inclusive but do not include extraneous material.

For each essay that you write, be as issue-inclusive as possible. Take care, however, to address only the matters asked. Do not lose time by digressing, going off on tangents or inserting extraneous material for its own sake.

Use headings to add organization and cohesiveness to your responses.

Organize your answer according to headings (and even sub-headings) for each of the subject areas that the question touches on. Remember that your job in answering an essay question is to address only the issues that are raised by the question presented. Do not include irrelevant information or recite a run-on narrative for its own sake.

Put each heading in bold, to give your professor a helpful roadmap to your answer as well as lend an internal cohesiveness to your response. If you are running out of time, be sure to include, if only in bullet points, the additional issues that you spotted but won't be able to elaborate upon.

Do not be informal in tone and do not try to be humorous.

Humor is risky and likely to detract from the integrity of your response. Be formal in tone throughout. Avoid colloquialisms and be respectful in tone.

CHAPTER 51

Ten Quick Tips to Avoid Common Pitfalls

Exam-taking is a skill that improves with time and practice. To enhance your performance, keep in mind the following tips, intended to help you to avoid common, easily-remedied mistakes.

1.) Be sure to answer the call of the question.

The call of the question is what the exam is asking you to do with the given equation, fact pattern or excerpt presented. Answer the question(s) asked. Do not answer questions that are not asked. Do not waste precious time on tangents. Often, a student will lose points on an exam simply because he or she overlooked part of the call of the question, and failed to respond to one or more of the points asked.

2.) Be issue inclusive.

On an essay exam, get to all or as many of the issues that are presented as you can within the allocated time and space.

3.) Follow through and define relevant doctrine.

Be sure to articulate the meaning of any terms of art that you use. Define pertinent doctrines and concepts.

4.) Organize your response.

Take time to outline and organize your answer. Use headings to lend an internal cohesiveness to your response. Ultimately, the substance of your answer is far more important than its form. Still, a cogent, orderly and organized format is a great plus. If you are hand-writing your exam, be sure to write legibly. To enhance overall readability, skip lines and write on every other page.

5.) Do not restate the question for its own sake.

Your professor knows the question(s) asked. Rather, apply your mastery of the material to the question(s) presented.

6.) Do not present vague, run-on kitchen sink narratives of extraneous material.

Be selective and discerning in your use of relevant passages from the materials assigned.

7.) Make value judgments.

Sift the relevant material from the irrelevant, and respond ethically and professionally.

8.) Do not surrender your common sense.

Think about and note the practical implications of the result that you are exploring.

9.) **Budget your time and do not exceed the recommended time limit for each question.**

This is perhaps most important of all. Carefully establish a time budget for each exam question and honor that budget. You will be penalized for failure to get to a question. Force yourself to move on once the allotted time for a given question has run out.

10.) **Once the exam is over, let it go and move on.**

Do not get weighed down by second-guessing yourself or doing *post-mortems*, particularly when you have another exam to prepare for.

CHAPTER 52

When it All Seems Like Too Much to Do

It does not have to be perfect.

When it all seems like too much to do, realize that is probably because you are holding yourself to an unrealistic standard of perfection. Abandon the quest for some brand of nuanced excellence that you have conjured up and simply commit to doing well enough. Well enough is good enough.

All you need to do is cross the finish line.

You do not have to come in first, second or even in the top 99%. The last one to cross the finish line still crosses the finish line. Every finish brings you closer to the dream. Take your time and cross the line.

Trust that it will all be worth it.

Even if it seems a leap of faith right know, know that you are precisely where you are meant to be. All of your hard work will be worth it and it will be rewarded.

Be a counter of blessings rather than a collector of grievances.

Cultivate a persistent mindset of great gratitude. You have been given a chance that most people around the world would do anything to have.

When a self-defeating thought pops up, *choose another thought.*

Keep in the forefront of your mind one particular experience from the past that made you feel successful. Maybe it was a graduation day, an outstanding performance on your part or some context in which you felt confident and in control. Remember it with as much detail as you possibly can. When a self-defeating doomsday thought comes creeping in, replace it with that happy memory.

You are in charge of your thoughts. Your thoughts are not in charge of you.

When panic or dread comes up, notice the thought that immediately preceded it. Test the veracity of that thought. By critically examining the thought that led you to feel overwhelmed, you are switching from emotion mind to rational mind. In your rational mind, ask whether that thought is true. For example, suppose that you realize that the thought that precipitated your feeling swamped and exhausted was, *"I'll never get all this done,"* or *"I'll never understand this."* Those absolute, blanket characterizations tell you that you are in emotion mind, and your emotion mind can be a liar.

Remember that feelings are not facts. They are often fear-based and irrational. Instead of indulging those internal terror mongers, think, *"Baby steps. I can climb this mountain one small step at a time. When I get to material that I do not understand, I will mark it and later call a classmate or, if time permits, ask the professor about it. My work does not have to be perfect. I just need to do well enough, and I can do that. I will stick with this for the next three hours, and then I am going to take a break and watch a How I Met Your Mother rerun and eat peanut butter cup ice cream."* Your energy level will perk up after that pep talk. Proceed to put in the time that you promised yourself you would, and then take the much-deserved break that you promised yourself you would take.

CHAPTER 53

Once the Exam Is Over, Let It Go and Move On

Let it be.

You may have a temperament that makes it difficult for you to let things go. Your tenacity can be a blessing, but sometimes it will not serve you well. When it comes to exams, once the exam is over *let it go*. Do not engage in after the fact de-briefing with classmates. Most often, that will make you feel unsure of what you did or did not do. Do not waste time after an exam by going back to your books to double check your responses. Move on, particularly if you have another exam to prepare for.

When you start to get pangs of anxiety over what you think you did or did not do on the exam, switch the thought. Say to yourself, *"No, no, no, I like you too much to have you beat yourself up right now."* And then resume your focus on the task at hand.

The ring around the bathtub remains.

Think of exam preparation as filling a bathtub. The water represents all of the information and material that you need to get into your head to get through the exam. When the exam is over, unplug the drain and let the tub empty. What remains is the ring, or core essentials that will stay with you for years to come. You must empty the tub to be able to fill it for the next exam. Do not let the old water stagnate. Let it go.

CHAPTER 54

On Grades

You are not your grades.

No grade has the power to define you, chart your course or set your limits. Only you have that power. Decide that the world is yours, and it is.

School modes of evaluation leave much to be desired. In contexts where often there is little feedback, how one happens to do on a particular day on a two or three hour test tends to take on an undeserved importance and magnitude. Some even construe their grades as the final word on their abilities and future opportunities. Nothing could be further from the truth.

Intelligence is multi-dimensional and your unique range of intellectual, practical and emotional aptitudes is mightier than any number or letter ascribed to some linear metric of your proficiency. That vast range, coupled with your tenacity and heartfulness, is the best predictor of your success and your significance in the world.

Your grades, whatever they happen to be, are an indication of how well you fared in applying your learning to a narrow format, as determined by an inevitably arbitrary and often subjective judgment. In this imperfect system, injustices and unexpected outcomes are inevitable. People who hardly studied may excel. The course that you thought you aced could represent your worst grade. The exam that you thought you bombed could come back as your best grade. And so on.

Let your grades inform your life, not define, diminish, or even exalt it.

You are not your grades. Do not, even for an instant, submit to the misperception that any grade defines who you are and what you are capable of. To see how crazy that would be, imagine that you are told that you will be tested and graded on the sweater that you choose to wear on a particular day. The instructions indicate that the sweater should be in a primary color. You come to the "test" wearing a bright blue sweater. You thought about that choice in advance, and it seemed appropriate. You are graded on that choice, and the grade comes back a B. When you ask why, you are told that wearing red would have earned you more points, and that sweaters with buttons fared better on this test. That B does not tell a "truth" about you, your ability to dress yourself or your capacity to follow instructions. It does not even reveal any "truth" about the "worthiness" of the sweater that you picked. It is a perfectly good sweater. At best, giving the testing process every benefit of the doubt, it tells about the merits of your sweater choice on that particular day. More likely, it indicates that the grader in subjective judgment prefers red to blue in the palate of primary colors.

Do not give any grade a significance that it does not deserve. Think of each grade as someone's opinion about the choices you made on a particular day. There are few absolutes in this realm and certainly many opportunities to be self-corrective. You will get better at exam-taking the more times that you have the opportunity to go into the metaphorical closet and select a sweater.

Repetition is the key to mastery.

Grades are simply a means of feedback, letting you know whether you have figured out how to play the exam-taking game. If your grades are not what they should be, take the offensive and seek out people and resources to help you to improve your exam skills. Consult with each of your professors. Find a tutor. Speak with upper-class students who have done well in the given courses you are now preparing for.

A few weeks before the semester ends, begin taking practice exams. Some of your professors will have their past exams on file. When that is the case, ask your teachers to critique your work on those practice tests. That process, albeit tedious, is immensely helpful first because it hones your "muscle memory," or your brain's capacity to store and then more readily access the skill set needed to perform well on the actual test. Second, by receiving your professor's comments, you get a better sense of what he or she values most and deems most essential.

Diversify your portfolio.

You have the power to dilute the significance of grades by demonstrating your excellence in other contexts. Become a student leader on campus. Write for the school newspaper. Do volunteer community outreach work. Take advantage of internship opportunities. Become a research assistant to a member of the faculty. Those are among the ways for you to create value, establish yourself as a capable contributor and shine.

Be thankful for every stride that you make.

As you do everything you can to enhance your performance, try to keep matters in perspective. Pace yourself, and know that time is on your side. The road is long. Be appreciative and grateful for the strides that you are making. Know that every step, however small, puts you that much closer to realizing your goal.

In life, what counts is *who* you are. The multitudes of aptitudes and attributes that you bring are uniquely yours and have an important place at the table.

Only you create the reality that your grades represent. No one else can do that. Throughout, keep your head high. Hold tight to your dignity, integrity, and belief in yourself. You are precisely where you should be. You have succeeded before. You will succeed now.

Your brand of excellence will be uncovered, recognized and valued. But first, you have to value it. Do not denigrate your brand. Cherish it. Believe in it. Be proud of it. With quiet confidence, rest assured that the world will follow your lead.

Think, act, and react as a successful, prosperous, and intelligent person would. Remember that what you think about most expands. What you think about most is what you move towards. Success is more attitude than it is aptitude. With your thoughts and attitudes, you are shaping the quality of your life.

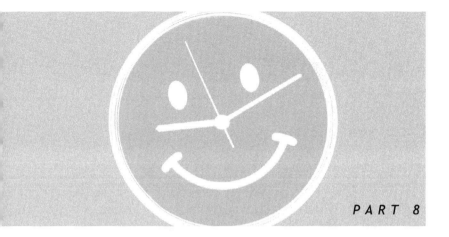

PART 8

How to Persist in Your Capacity to Love School, Your Work and Your Life

CHAPTER 55

The Pony

When I was in the sixth grade I was selected to participate in a national science fair. My project was based on the hypothesis that antibiotics could be grown from soil. I had several petri dishes filled with dirt, and mold and spores were growing in those plates. As I tried to figure out how those might become the stuff of penicillin, I had volumes and volumes of information piled up on the dining room table. Sifting through that material was tedious and often overwhelming. One night, as I sat there scratching my head, my dad must have sensed my growing despair.

My dad told me a story that he had heard on television. It is the story of a parent who has two children. One of the children is an avowed optimist, happy no matter the circumstances. The other is deeply pessimistic and cynical most of the time. The parent, trying to bring both children back to center, fills the pessimist's room with all of the toys and games known to delight even the fussiest child. By contrast, he fills the optimist's room with several pounds of horse manure, to help to teach the child that sometimes life just stinks.

The parent waits ten minutes or so, and then ventures into the pessimist's room. He finds the child standing in a corner, arms folded in front of him, scowling. The boy says to the parent, *"How dare you patronize me with these petty offerings?"* Saddened, the parent heads to the optimist's room. There he is astonished to find his child busily spraying air freshener while shoveling the horse manure into a neat pile. The parent asks, *"Child, in the midst of all this, how can you possibly maintain so hopeful and cheerful an outlook?"* The child replies with great sincerity and strength of purpose, *"Daddy, don't you get it? With all this horse manure, there must be a pony here!"*

Do you see the analogy to your present circumstance? Amidst the volumes that you must shovel and store and sanitize, there are ponies. I promise you that. There will be joys and privileges in your chosen life's work that will astound and delight you. You have an important contribution to make, and it is uniquely yours. In the days ahead, do not let anyone or anything convince you otherwise.

Remember that life will meet you at your level of expectation for it. So will people. Keep your hopes high and look for the best in everyone and everything. It is there. Ask for the wisdom to see it.

To find love in the work that you do, put love into the work that you do. Tackle even the most mundane tasks with the precision and grace of the greatest maestro. Write the essay or paper with the assiduousness of the most fervent artists.

Make your work your art. Let others watch you with amazement as they ask, *"But why are you so happy?"* Smile and tell them, *"There's a pony coming."*

CHAPTER 56

In Summation: Quick Reminders to Stay on Point as a Student, Colleague and Citizen of the World

Lighten up.

When you feel burdened by the weight of the world, realize that you are probably taking yourself too seriously. In school, at work and throughout your lifetime you will get weighed down if you spend too much time worrying about what the grade will be or what others will think of you. Those worries are your ego talking. As my dear friend and colleague Andrea Schwartz often says, *"Your ego is not your amigo."* Stop buying into the group-think that tells you that your performance on exams or on any given task will somehow determine the rest of your life. Even as I type those words, they sound ridiculous. The choices that you make over the course of time will determine the rest of your life, not an exam, not a set of grades and not the outcome of any given assignment.

Remember that wisdom and compassion are indivisible.

Be kind. Respect intelligence, but respect decency even more. Everyone deserves respect, everyone has a story, and everyone has something to teach you.

Success is not the key to happiness. Happiness is the key to success.

Gratitude is the way to joy. No matter the adversity and incivilities that your life will sometimes be subjected to, you remain in charge of your reactions. A grateful heart does not have the room or the capacity to respond to meanness in kind. A spirit rich in appreciation for everything and everyone twinkles. It does not internalize the slings and arrows, because it knows that the boomerang effect must return those to their sender. *People get what they give.* Thus, give what you want to receive. Remember that a grateful person will always have more to be thankful about. A critic will always have lots to complain about.

Love your studies, your work and the people in your life.

Persist in loving them, even when they seem not to love you back. In life, you are who and what you love, and not who or what loves you. Love is always a choice. Choose it, again and again. Remember that the love part, at least at first, is easy. It is your capacity to persist in loving, even against all odds that will be the mark of your greatness.

What you think about and talk about most will expand.

However you define the world and your place in it, you will be right. Take care to seek out the good and to speak out the good. Be passionate and persistent in your praise of others. Be guided by what you admire and not by what you detest. Look for the high-minded, read about the heroic, and talk about the acts of courage, big and small, that you observe. Speak the truth directly and with compassionate honesty, not brutal honesty. There is too much brutality in the world. Let the words that you choose promote understanding. Do not participate in gossip, mean-spirited humor or name-calling. Avoid sarcasm, which is weakness in disguise.

Avoid labels.

The imposition of a label (as in, my "opponent," "enemy," "liberal," "conservative" and so on), shuts the door to the world of variations, possibilities and surprises that the reserving of judgments lets in.

You are not what you are called. You are what you answer to.

Take the time to answer for yourself the question, *"Who do you think you are?"* Otherwise, the world will try to answer for you. You are not an automaton, technocrat or hired gun. You are the rule of reason's best hope, the face of compassion and a voice for those who have yet to find their own. Answer to that.

The time to be happy is right now.

Happiness is not the end but *the means* to a greater good. Your joy serves the world. Keep close the people, experiences and things that bring you gladness.

Your life will take you to great heights. But no matter the altitude, honor your roots and be true to your first principles.

Remember who you are and where you come from. Honor the legacy that brought you to this place and time. Embrace a vision that deems the world noble and honorable.

Urge others to awaken from the slumber of complacency and do what needs to be done with the time that they have. By your example, teach that gentleness comes from strength.

Know that you come to every room to heal the room. In the face of need and despair, you heal with one generous impulse rendered one day at a time. You heal when you choose to love, and persist in loving, the promise of your life and the people, constituencies and causes that you are fortunate enough to serve.

Most of all, you heal when you finally decide to love yourself so much that the spillover cannot help but bring joy to the world.

CHAPTER 57

A Closing Wish

My wish is that you wield the instrument of your life to close the gap between what is and what ought to be. The time is now to remember who you are and what you stand for and to show up, really show up, as a force for the good. Use your hard-earned expertise to give people hope. Because when all is said and done, if you can do that, well, that is something to be really happy about.

CHAPTER 58

A Letter to My Son

This book began as a set of letters that I wrote to my son Michael as he was about to begin Boston College. In the months leading up to his departure, and in part to help with my own worry and sadness at the idea of letting him go, I would write him a letter a day, and leave the letter on his dresser. The letters contained advice, inspiration and reminders of the mightiness of his destiny and how much he is loved. They represented everything that I wanted him to know as he entered this next phase of his life. As the letters piled up, my son said, *"Mom, you should write a book."* This is that book.

Set forth on the next page is one of the letters to Michael that he selected for inclusion here.

August 12, 2011

Dear Michael,

As you begin this journey, take with you the best parts of home. Let those live in your heart and remind you of how very much you are loved and cherished. Now, you must remember to cherish yourself. Make choices worthy of the virtue that preceded you and the destiny that awaits you.

We suffer sometimes because we forget. Do not forget who you are and Whose you are. You come from a legacy of faith, discipline and compassion.

See the good in everyone because it is there. Know that everyone has something to teach you. Continue to be of service. Every day, vow to leave each and every place on your path better because you were there.

And Michael, never give up on love. It takes courage to believe in love, because sometimes it will knock you off your feet. But choose to love deeply anyway. Know that a heart that sometimes breaks has more room. Trust that God is expanding you with every joy and sorrow.

All that you will be lies ahead. Let the experiences that await be based on the mighty foundation of all that you are. You are a child of God, a champion of the underdog, a giver of hope and a vessel for grace to find its way. Most of all, you are loved. Let your work and your life be that love made visible. My darling son, set the world aflame!

I love you,

Mommy